Solo Walks

The First 100 Days

Rumi Koshino &
Alli Warren

RITE Editions.
San Francisco

I wish to begin this book by acknowledging and honoring the indigenous communities native to this region. I recognize the Ohlone, Ramaytush and Chochenyo people as the past, present, and future of this land.

On March 15th, 2020, when the shelter-in-place order was issued in San Francisco to prevent the spread of Covid-19, I began my daily practice of going for long aimless walks. I documented these walks with my phone camera and each day shared them though Instagram (@rumimirumiru).

As my sense of time expanded and shrunk and the ground solidified and disappeared, my mind also shifted from pandemic anxiety to the urgency of responding to the long existing, but now magnified system of anti-Black racism and social and economic inequity. And, so did the window signs, changing from "Everything will be OK" to "Defund the Police" and "Justice for Ahmaud Arbery, George Floyd, Breonna Taylor, Tony McDade, Elijah McClain..."

This book consists of the selected images from this experience, navigating through the first 100 days of solo walks, from the arrival of the coronavirus to the resurgence of the Black Lives Matter Uprising, along with the corresponding texts by the poet, Alli Warren.

Amidst all the chaos and hopelessness, the walks remind me of the persistent beauty of the everyday: the blooming Spring flowers, the colors of San Francisco houses, the golden hour shadows, the early evening sky and the children's sidewalk drawings. The BLM resistance and protests added another layer to my walks; they presented me with another kind of hope-filled beauty.

I walked without a specific direction in mind, and every walk gave me something of a joyful surprise. As the pandemic continues to worsen and the shelter-in-place continues, my solo walks continue.

I am extremely thankful to Robin Wright, Alli Warren and Margaret Tedesco for working with me to realize this special publication.

Rumi Koshino
August 2020

The First 100 Days

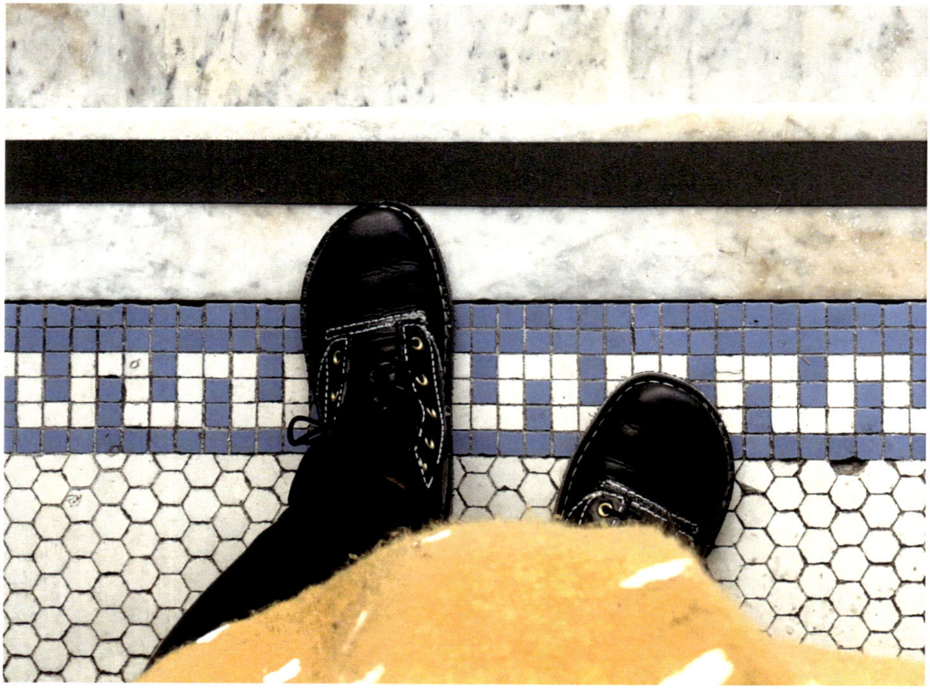

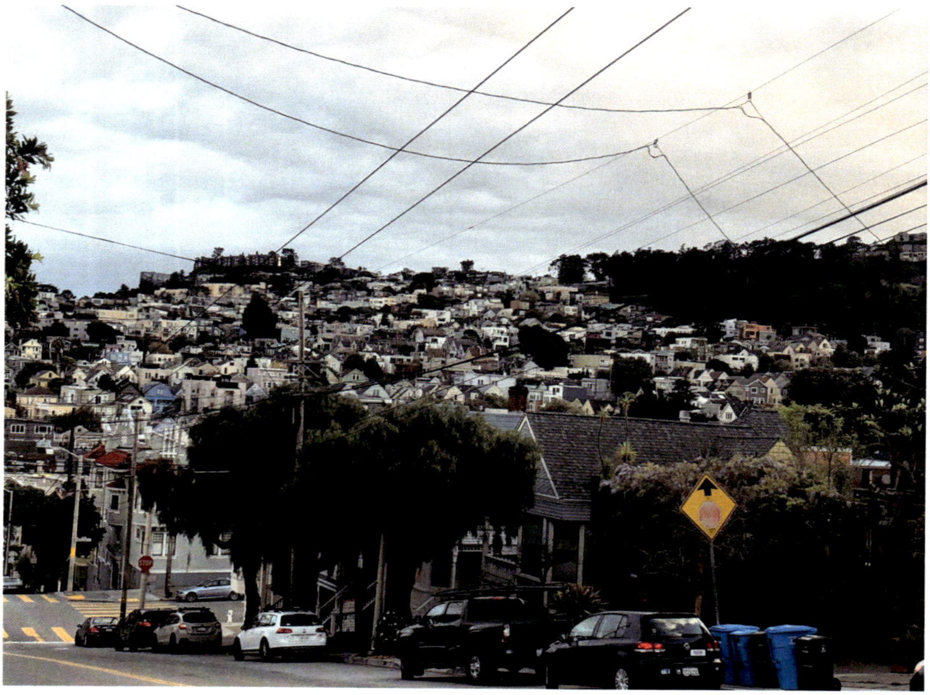

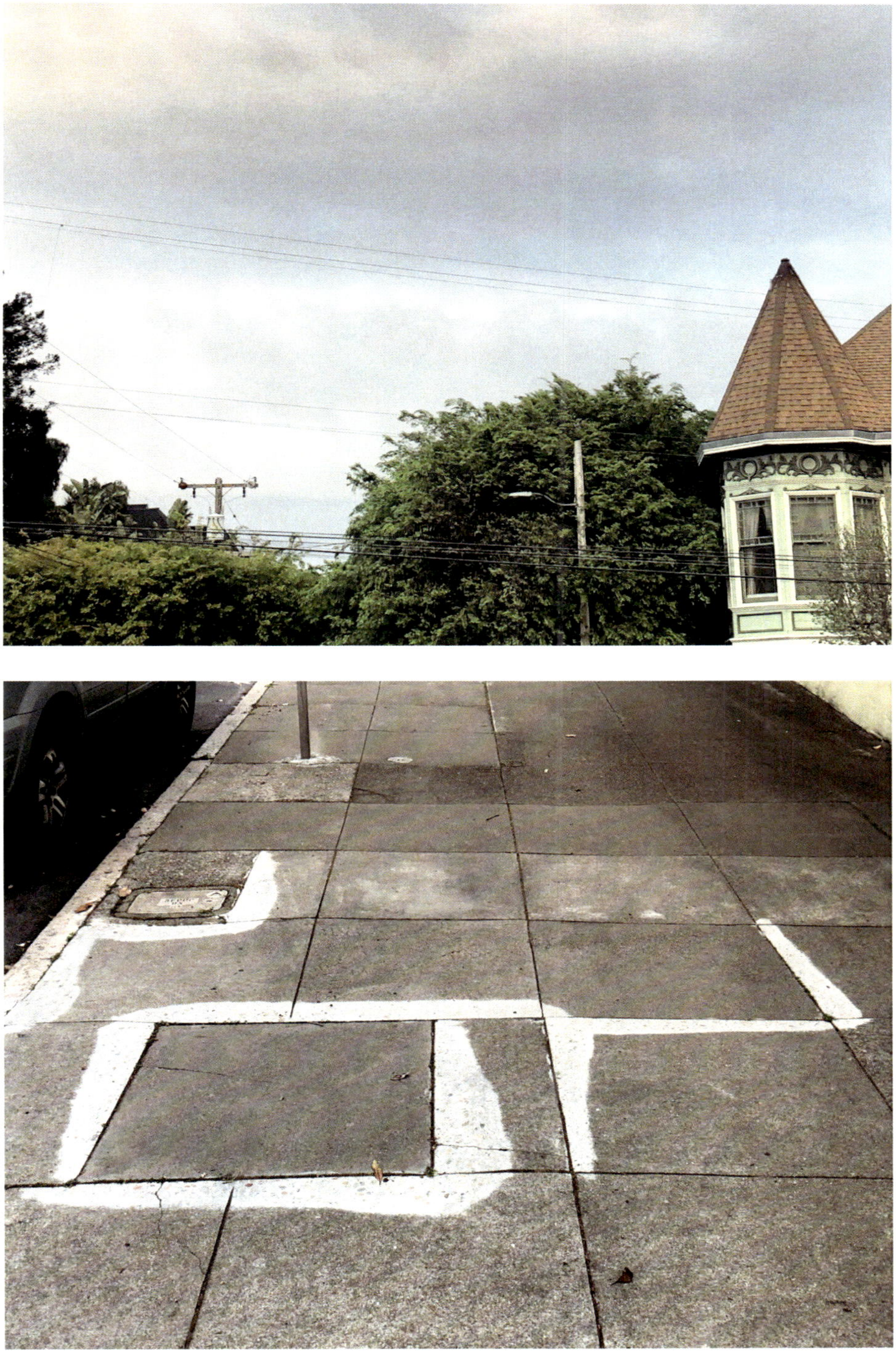

Sunday, March 15

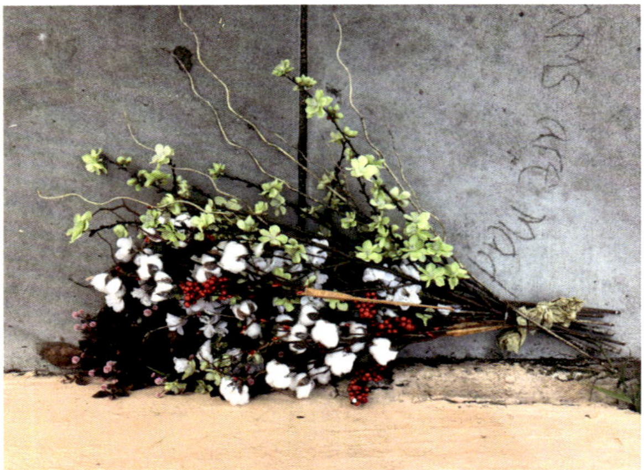
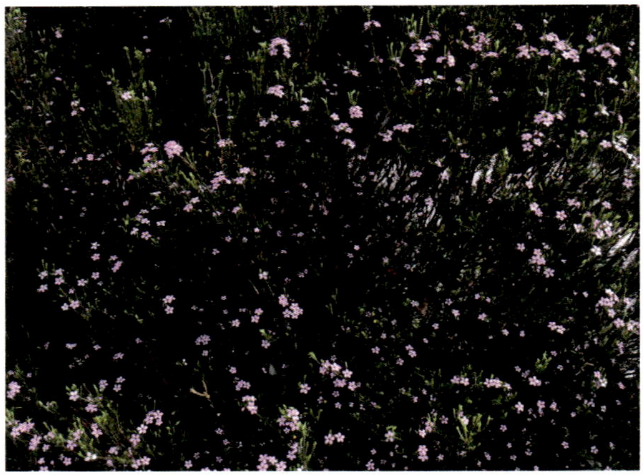
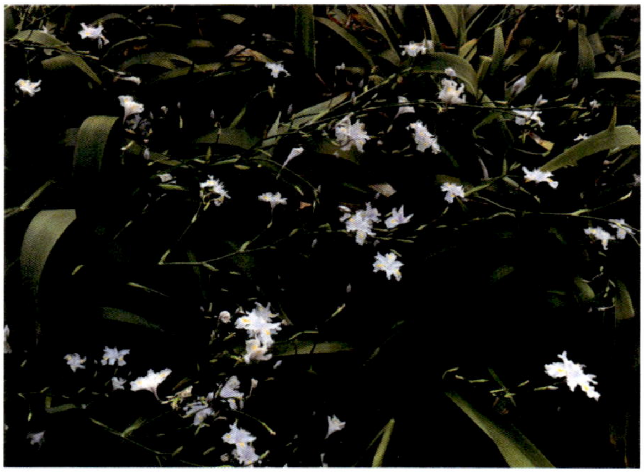
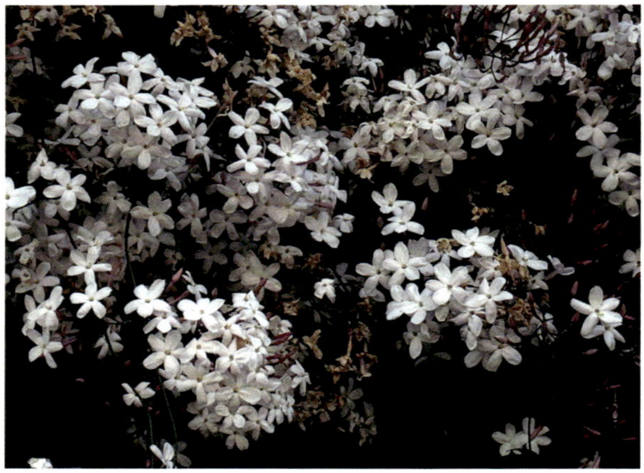
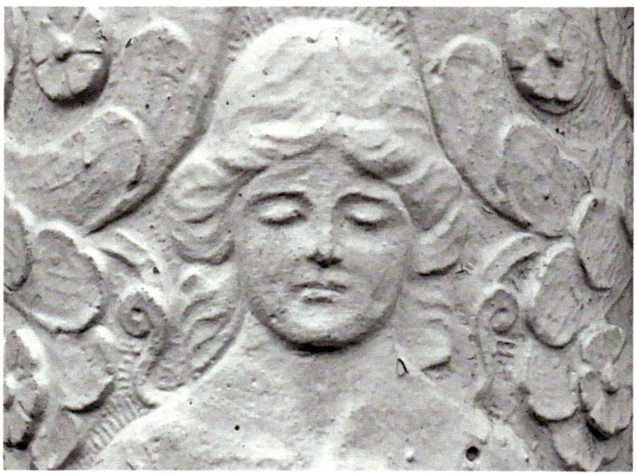
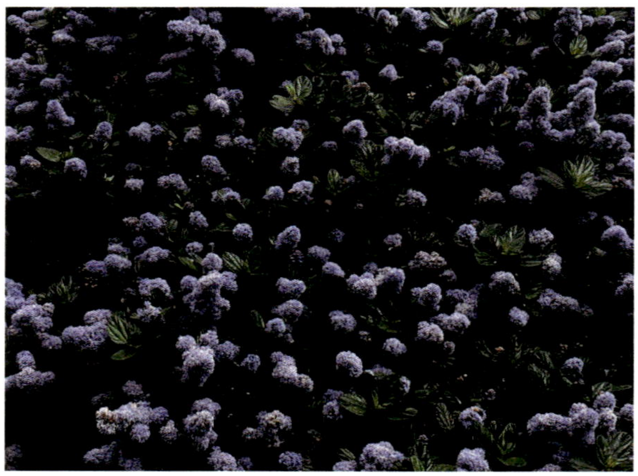

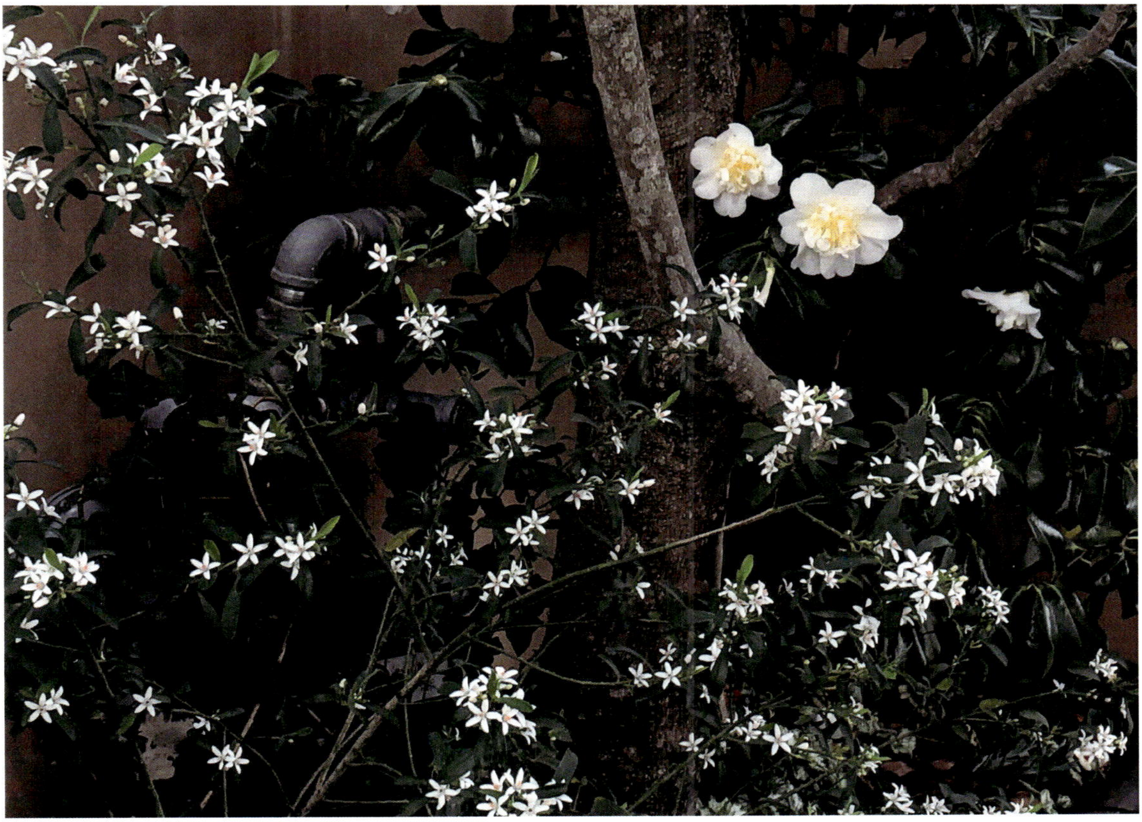

Friday, March 20

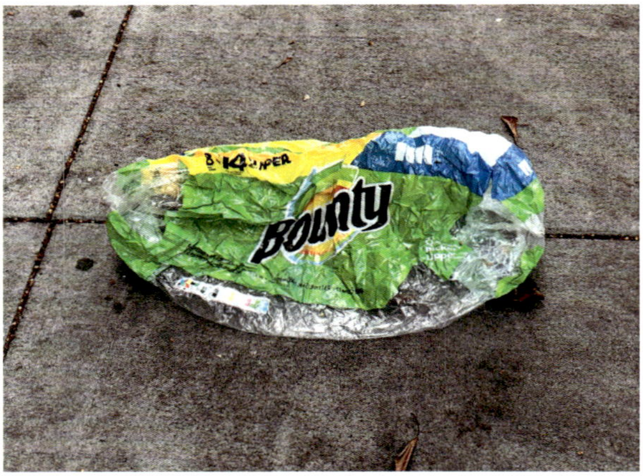
Bounty

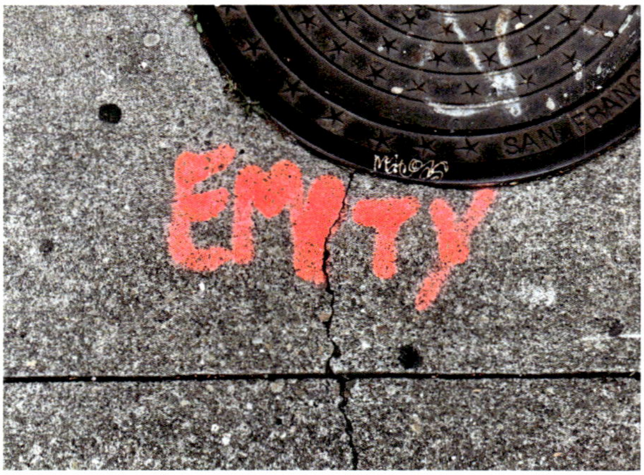
EMTY
SAN FRANC

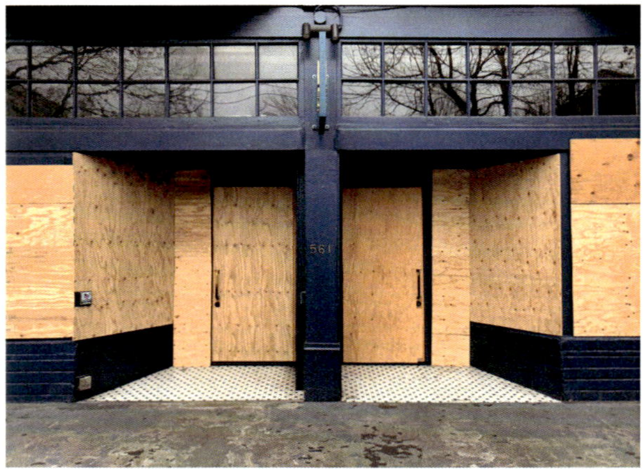
561

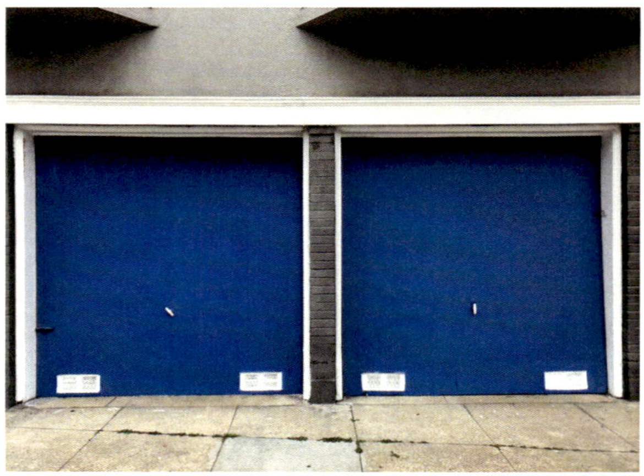

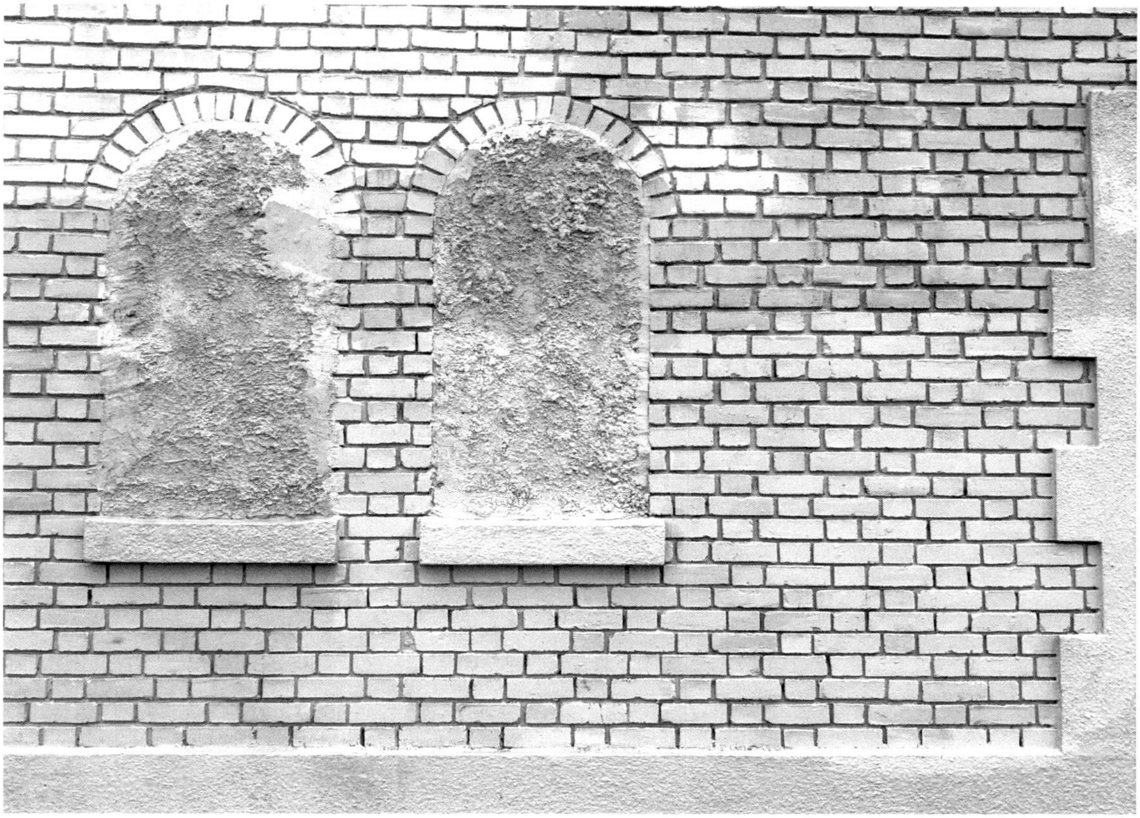

Monday, March 23

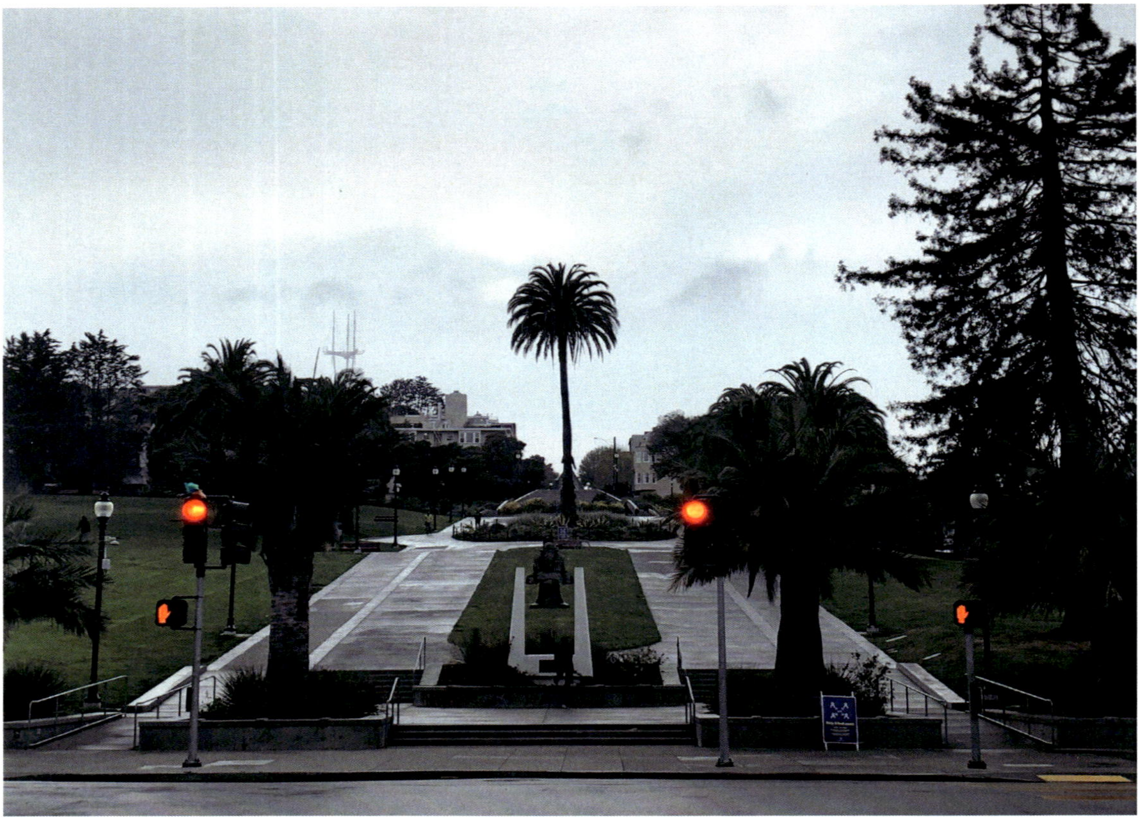

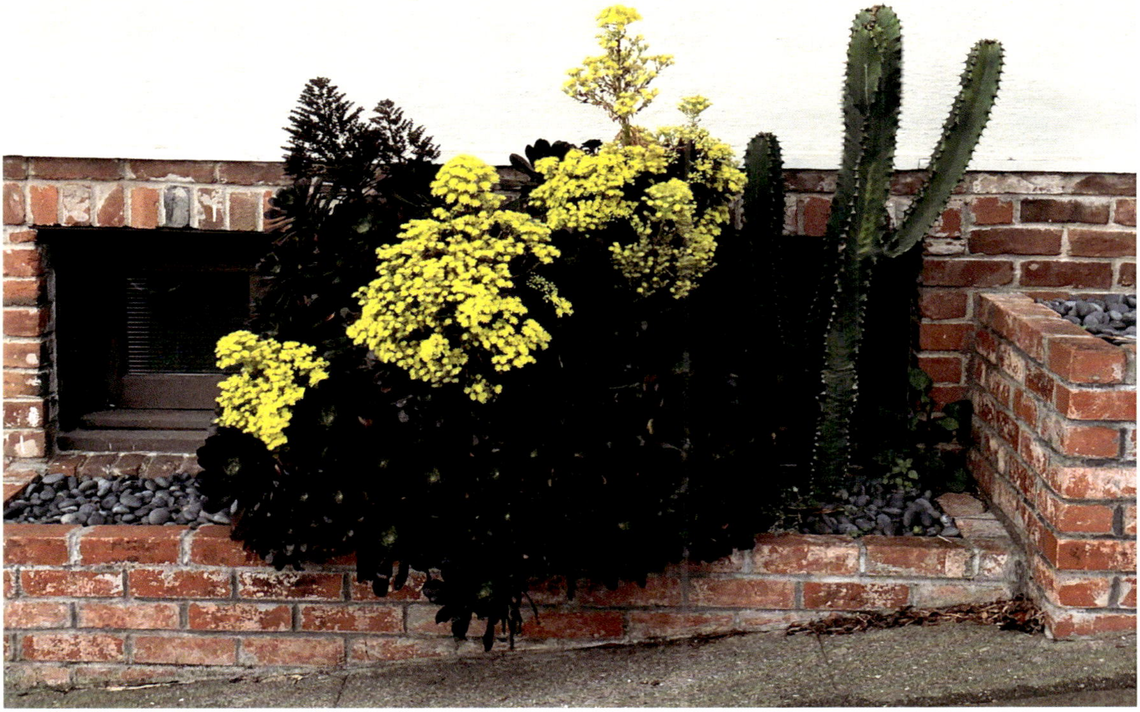

Saturday, March 28

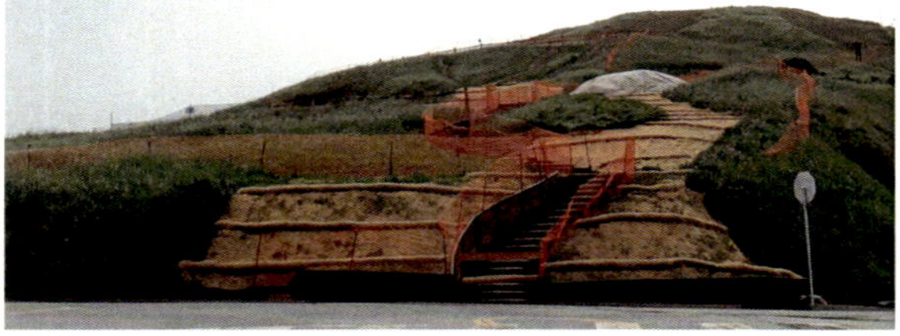

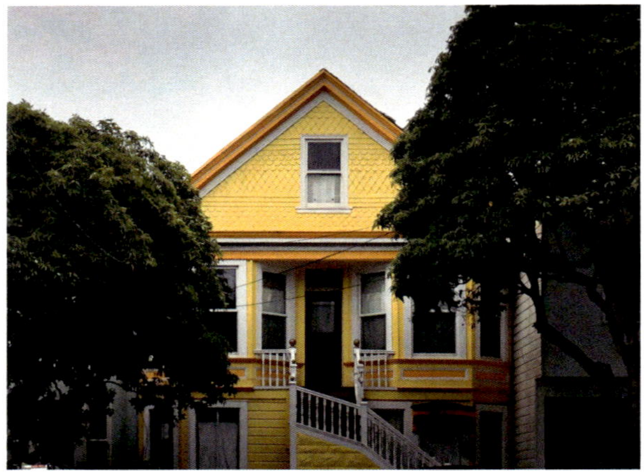

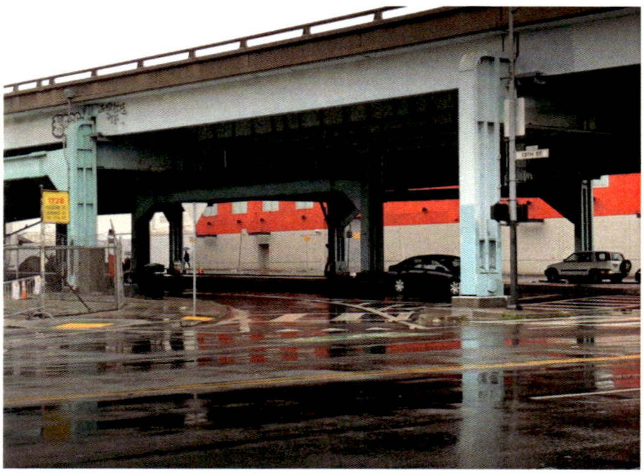

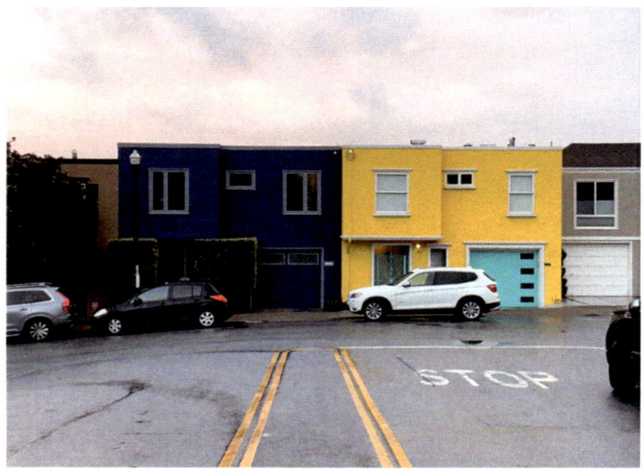
STOP

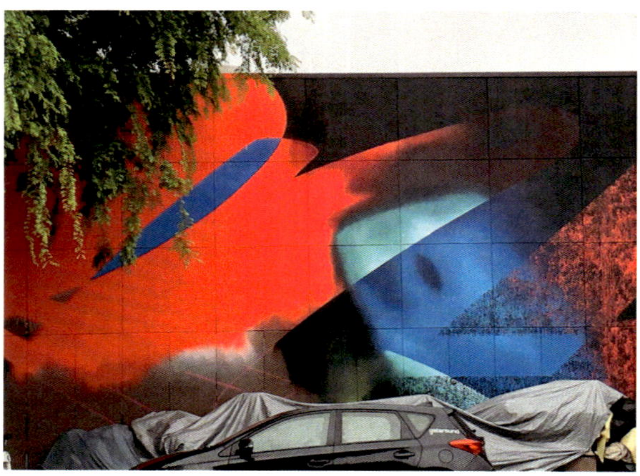

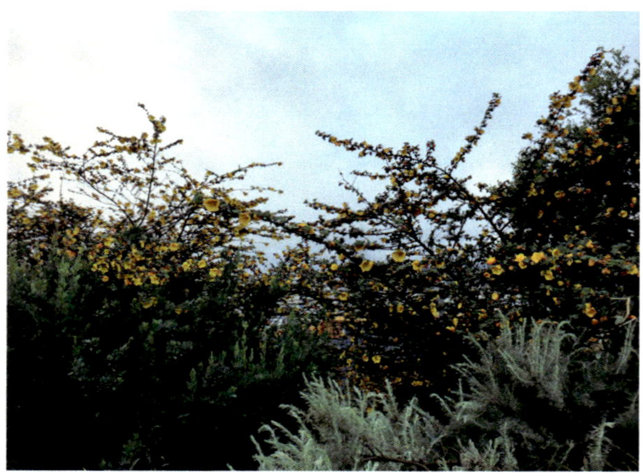

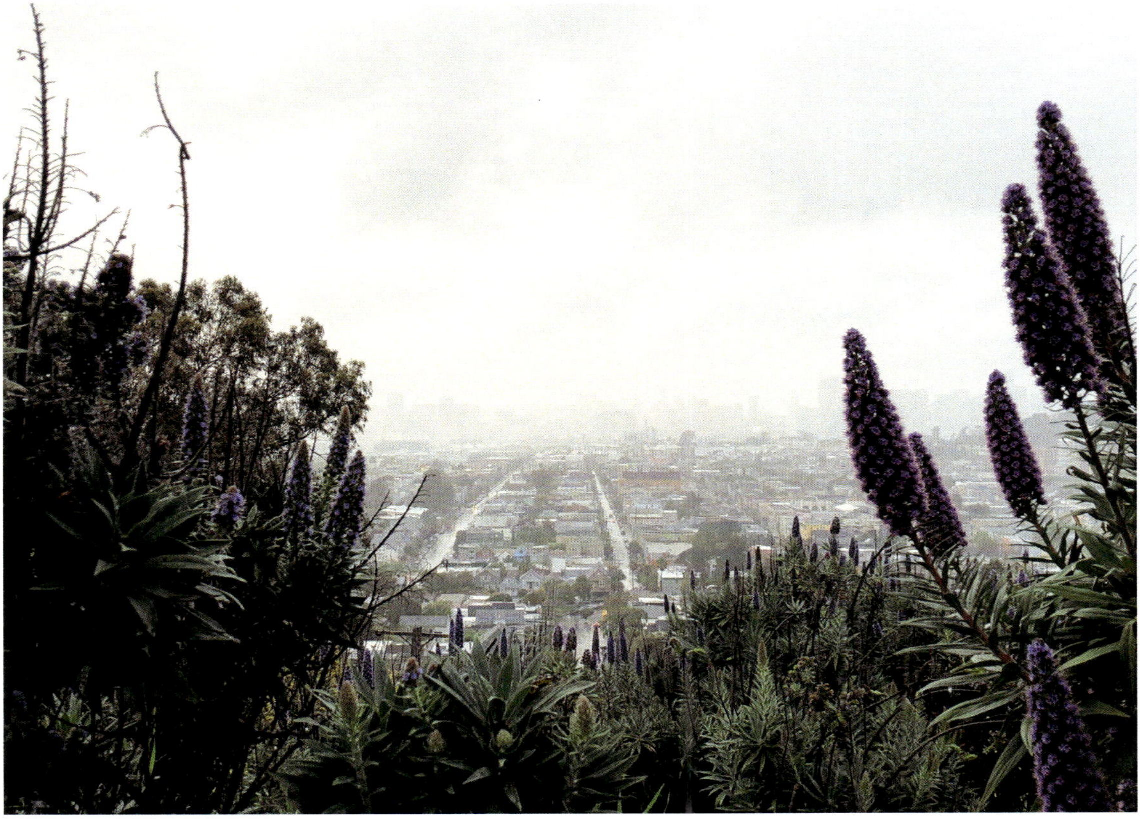

Saturday, April 4

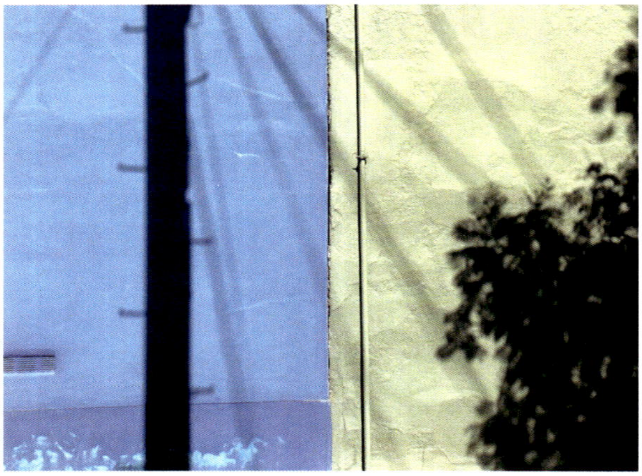

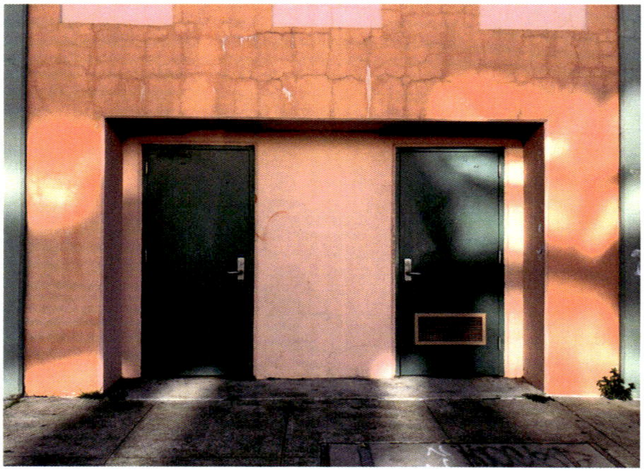

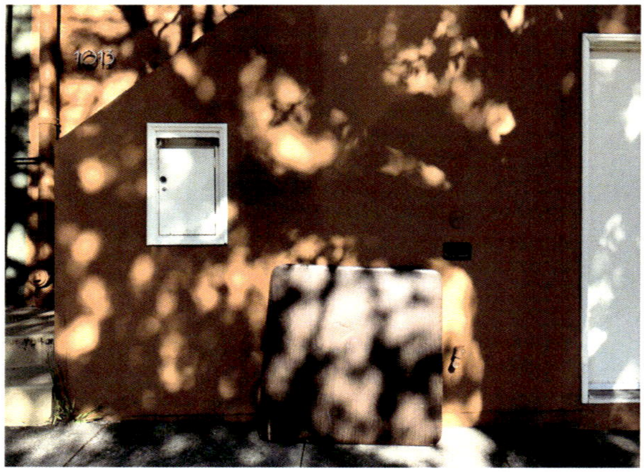

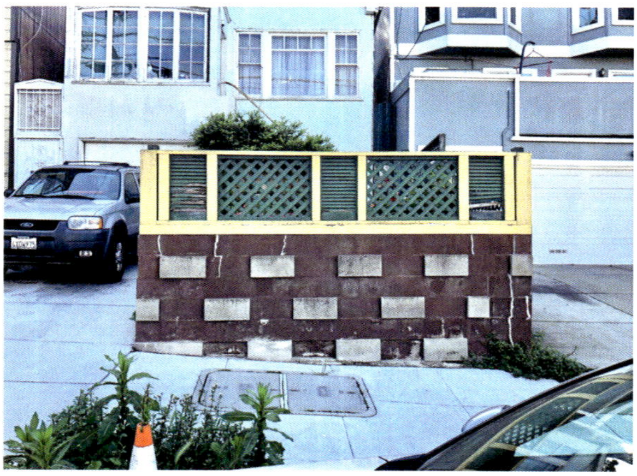

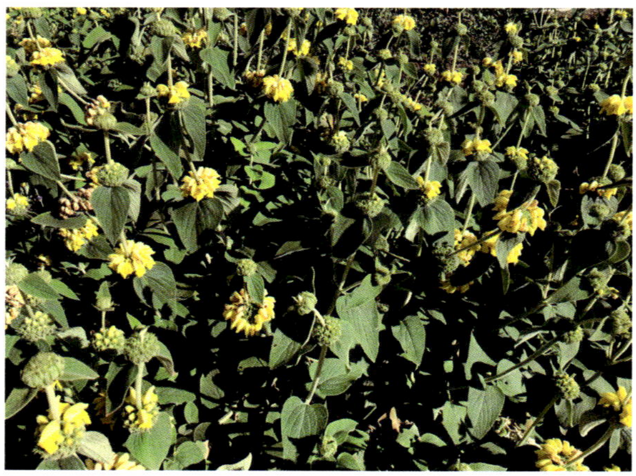

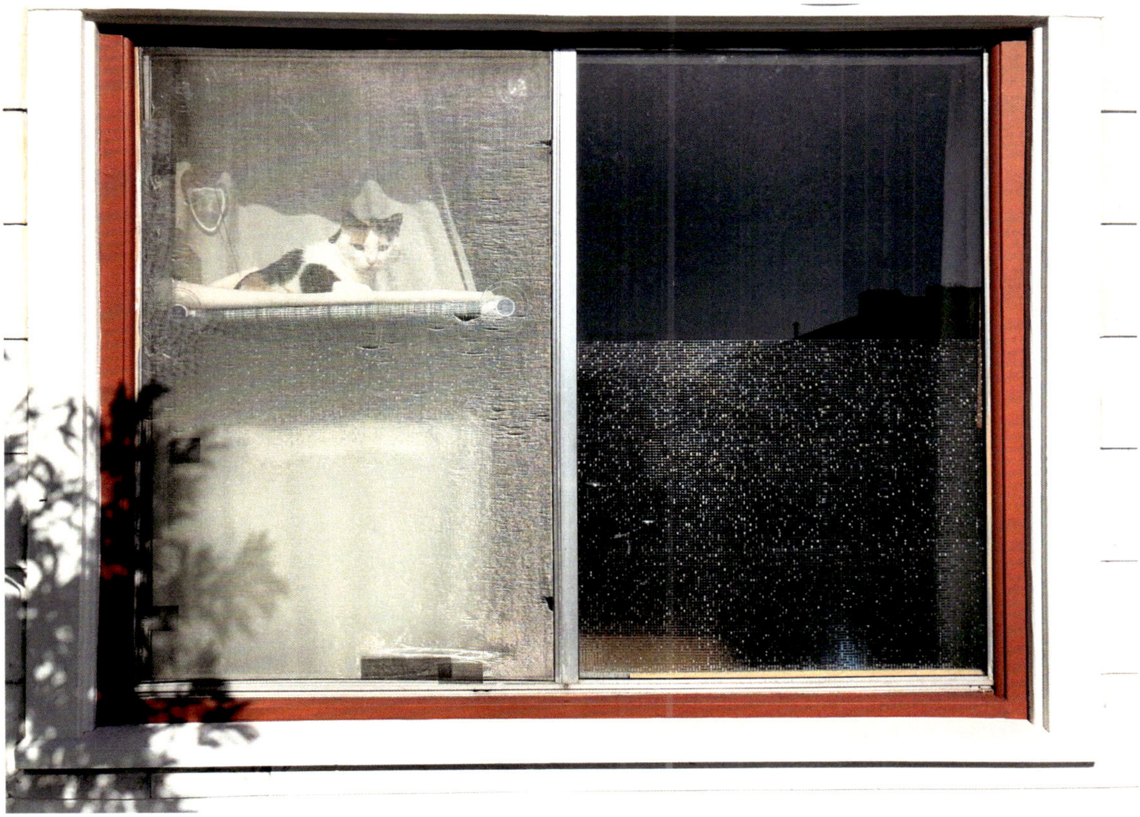

Monday, April 13

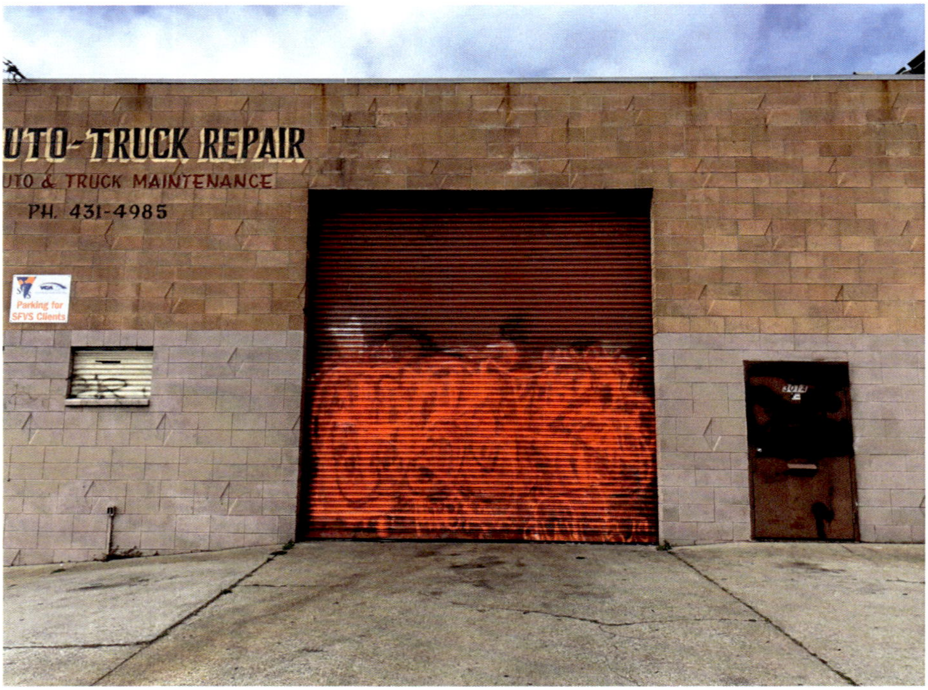
UTO-TRUCK REPAIR
UTO & TRUCK MAINTENANCE
PH. 431-4985
Parking for
SFVS Clients

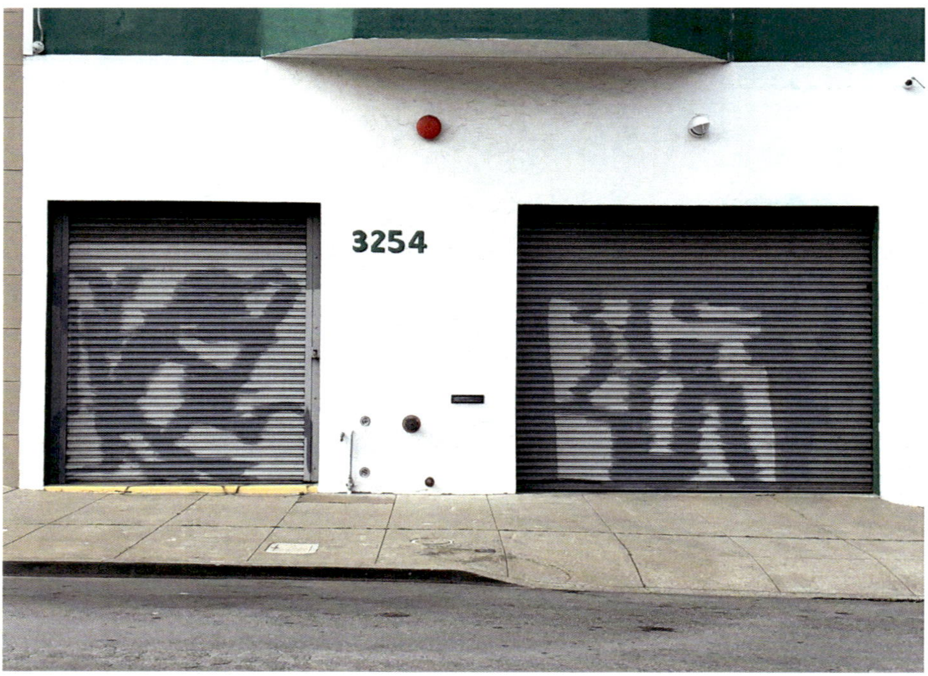
3254

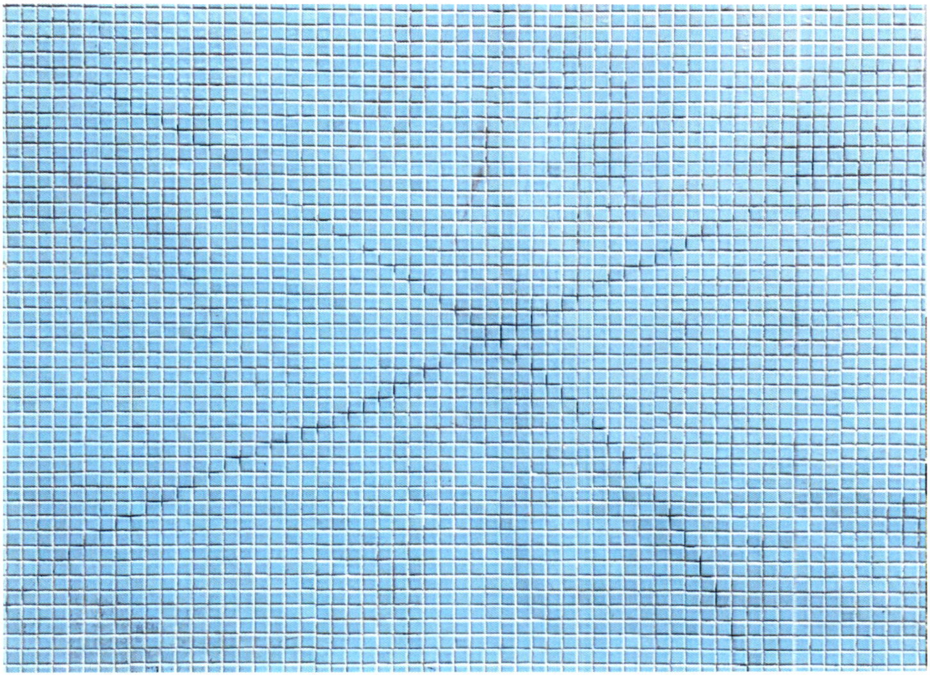

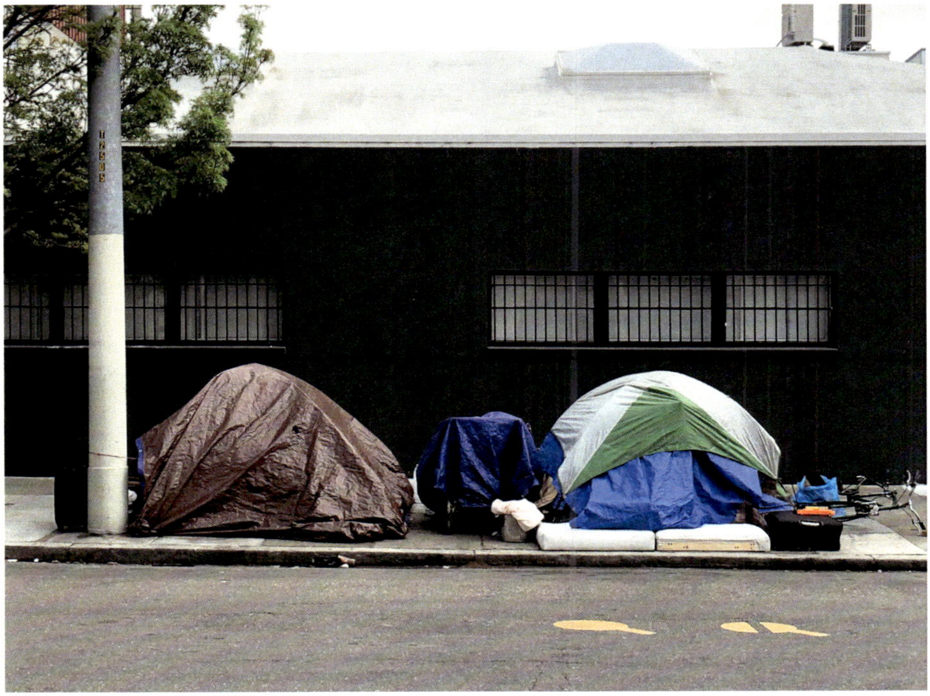

Thursday, April 16

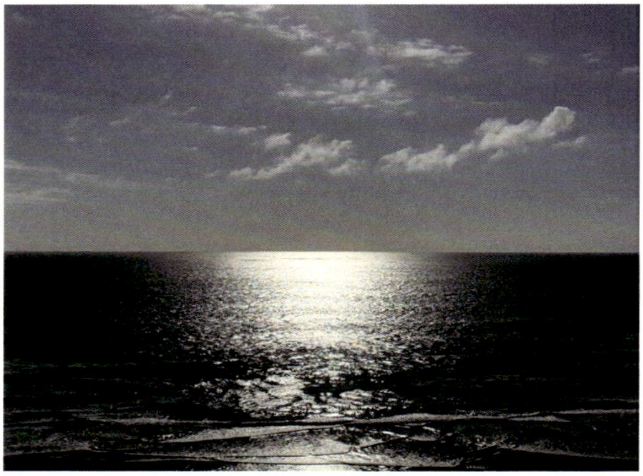

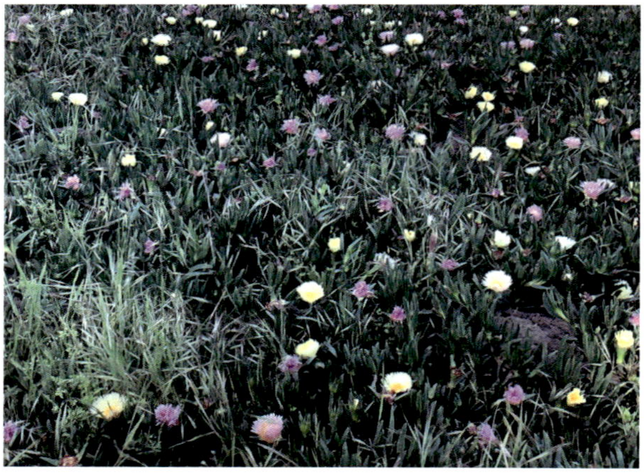

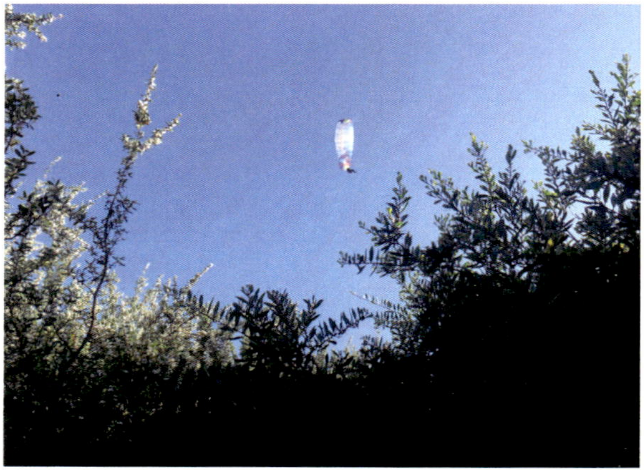

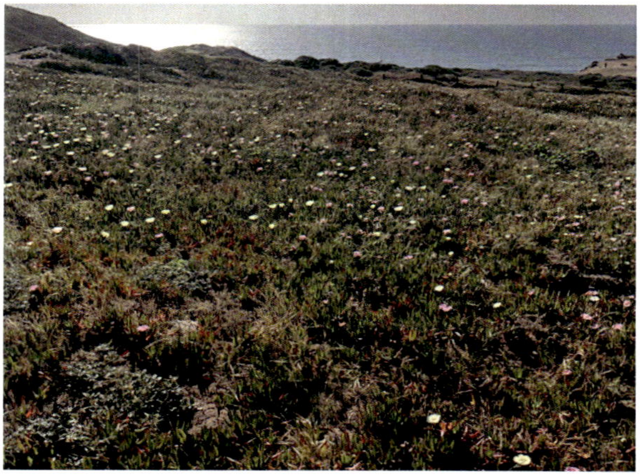

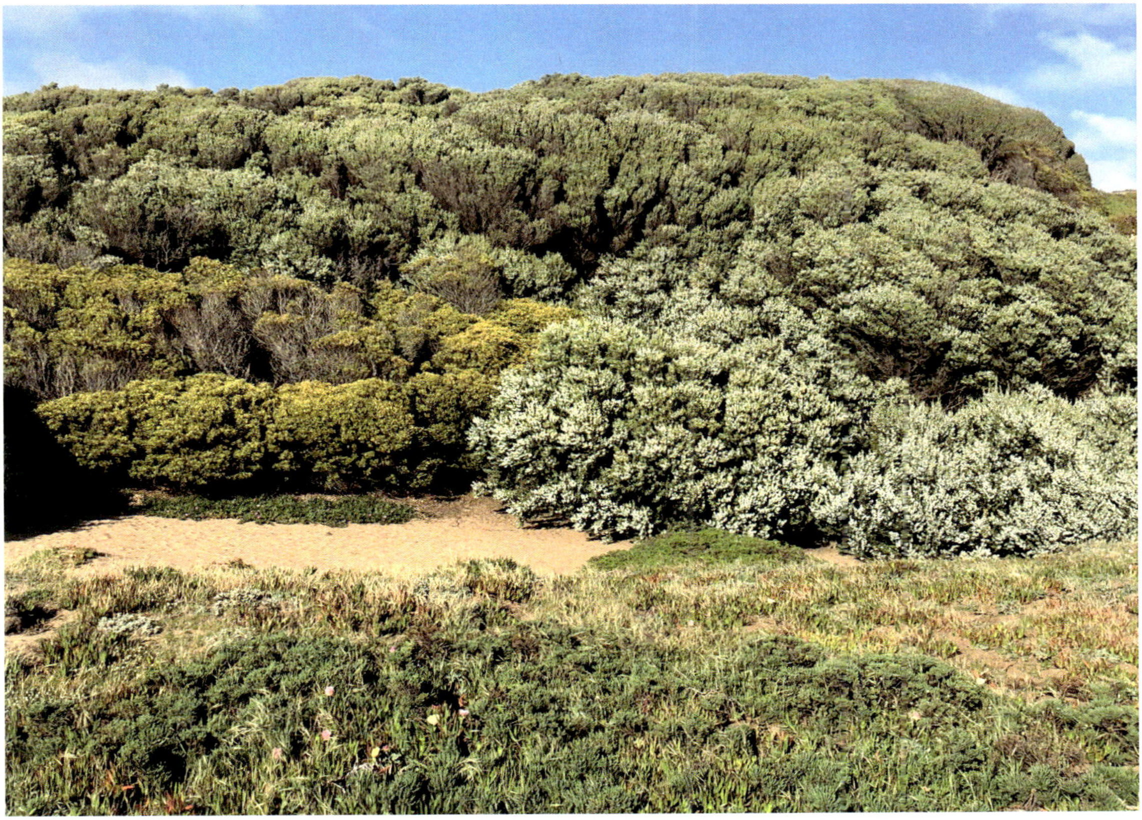

Saturday, April 18

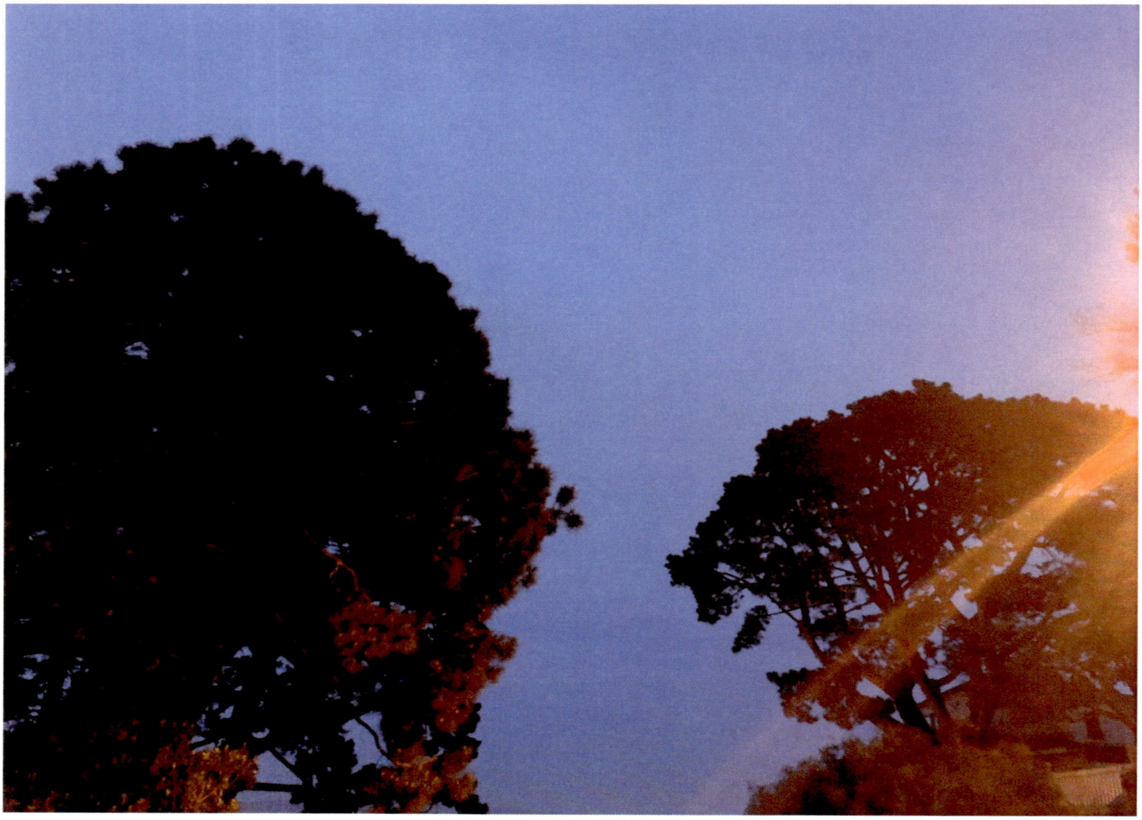

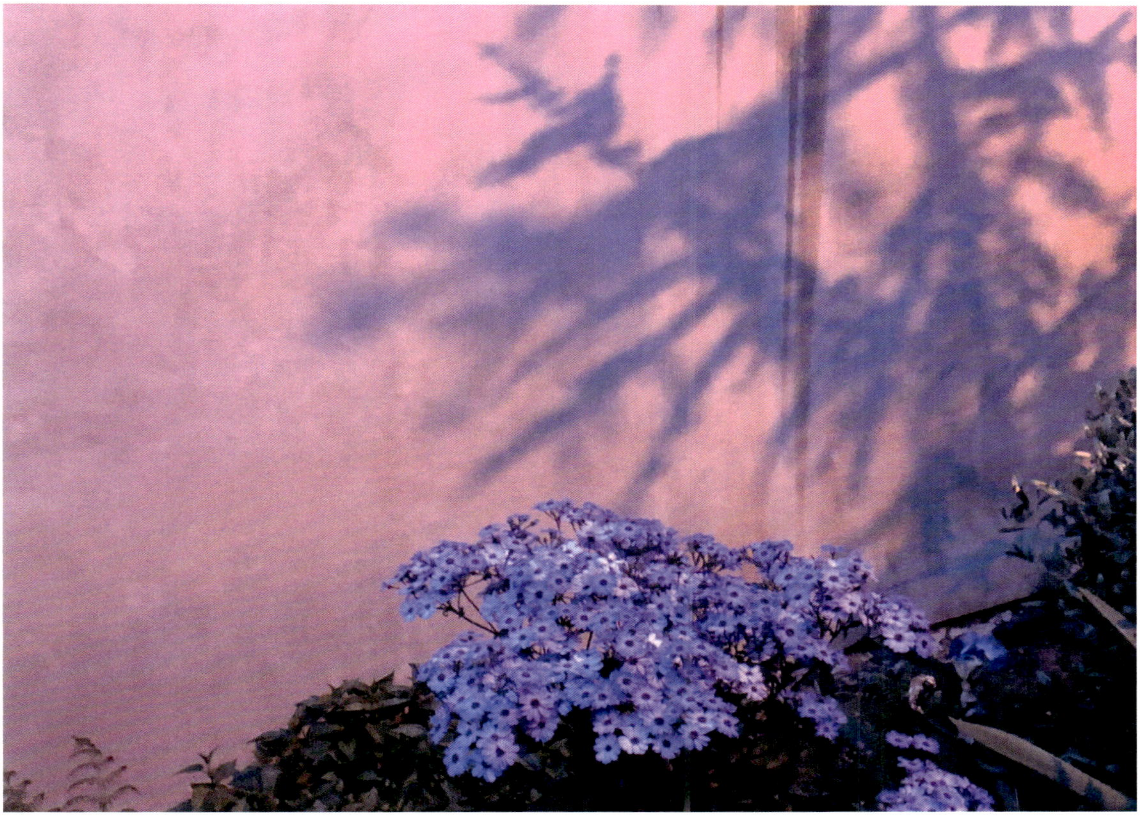

Sunday, April 19

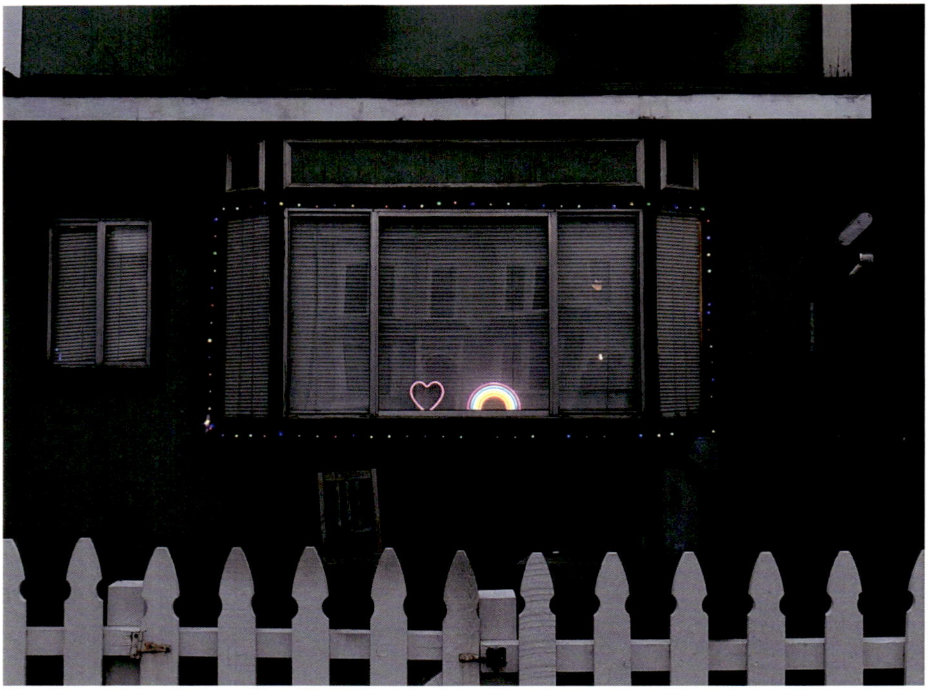

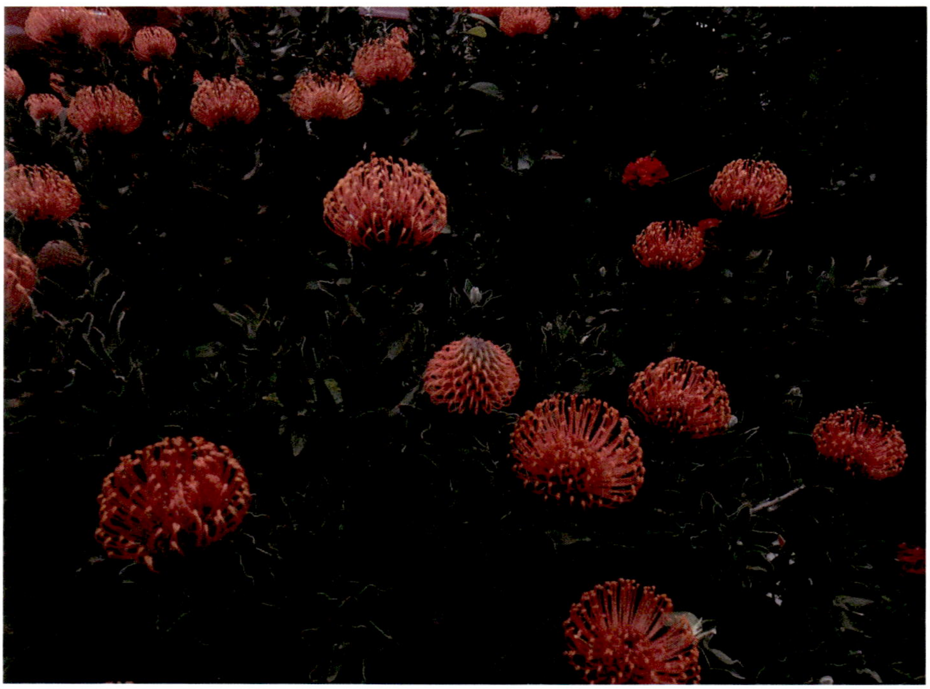

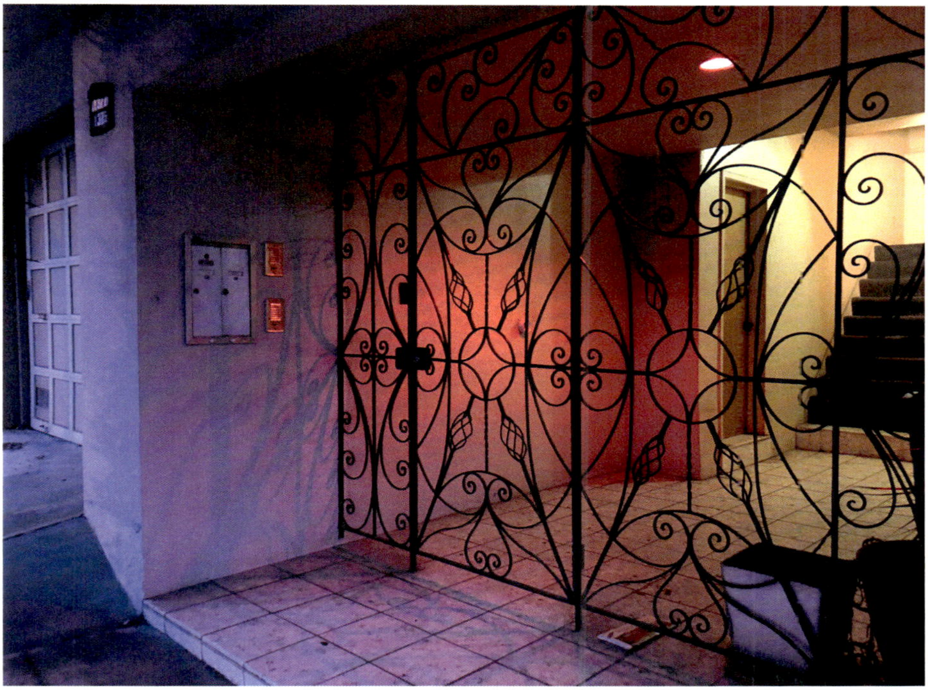

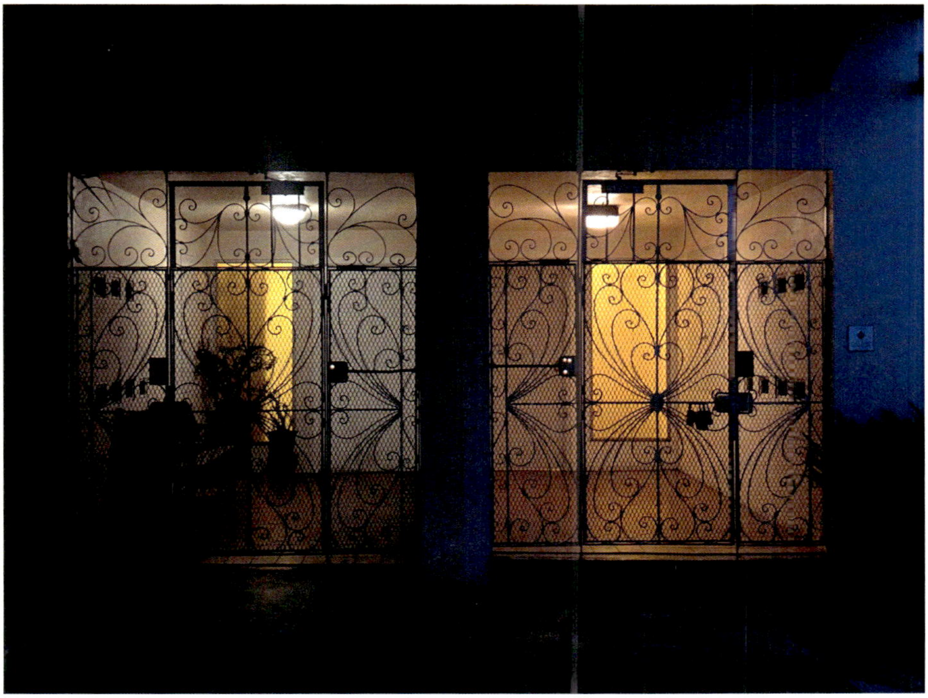

Monday, April 20

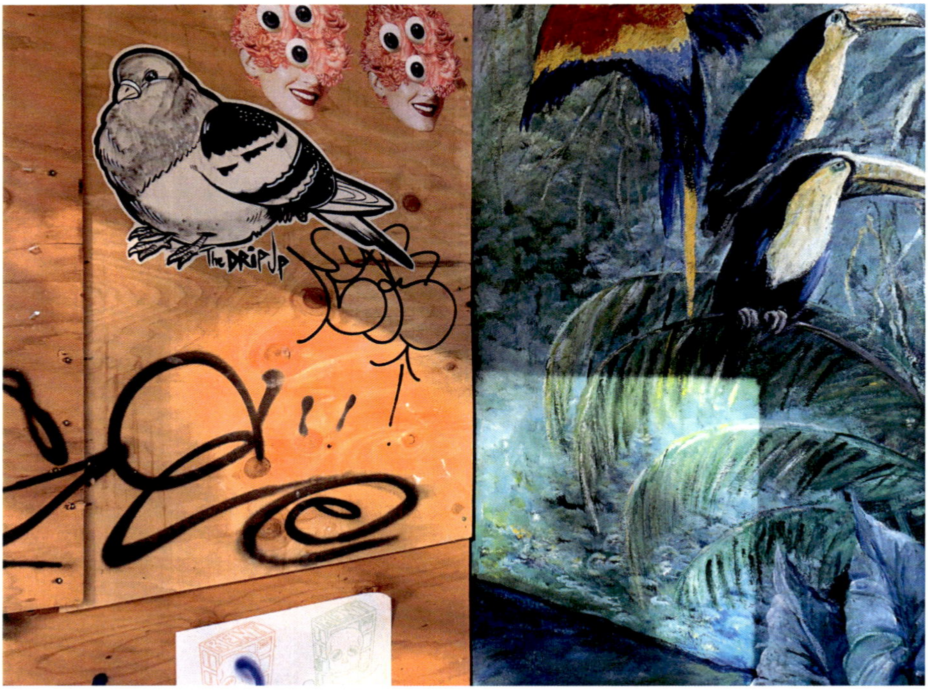
The DRIP Jp

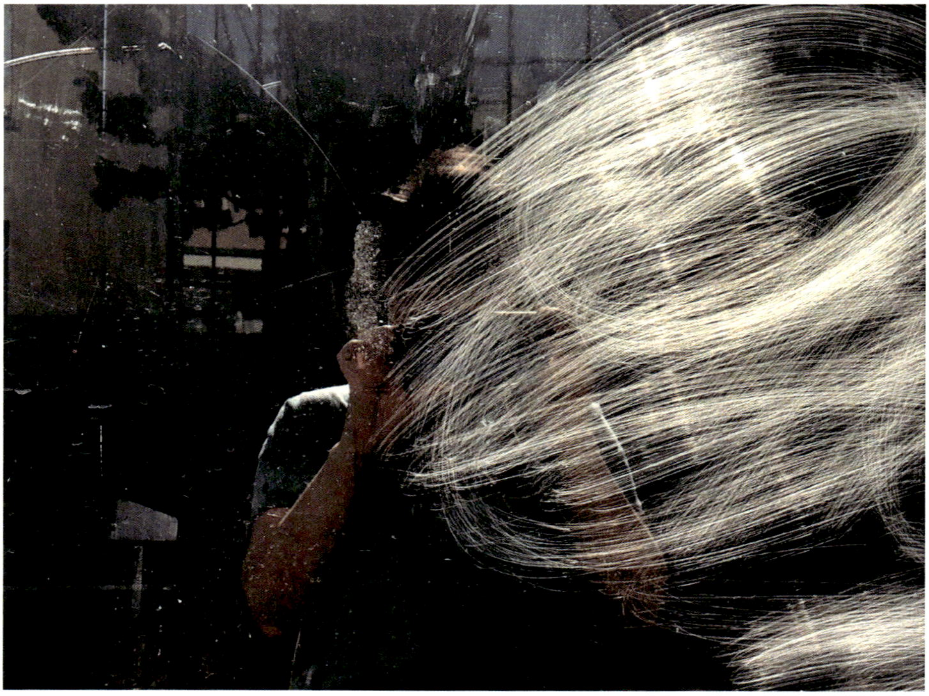

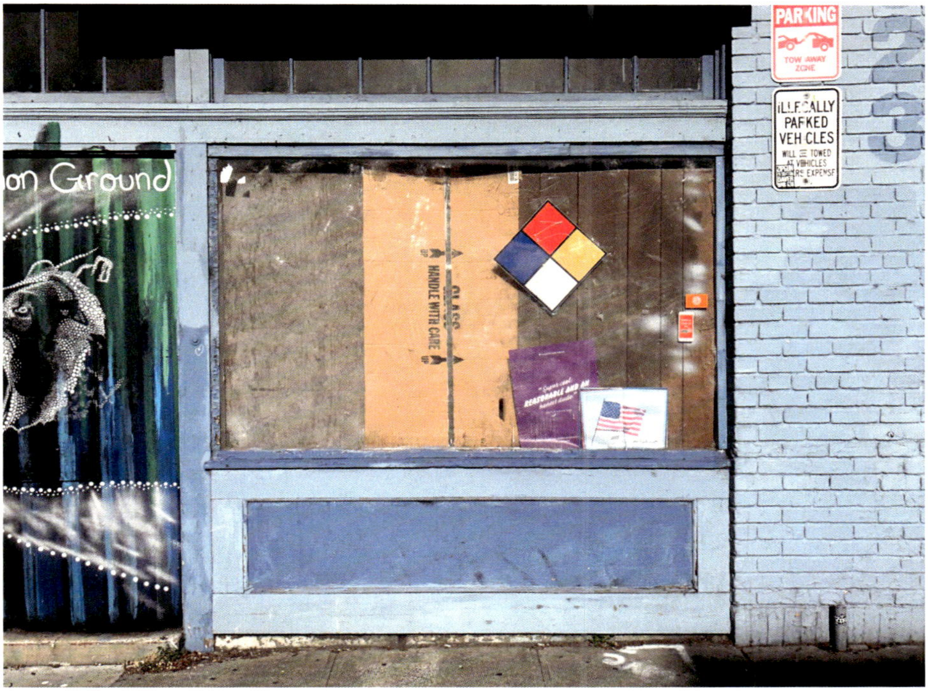

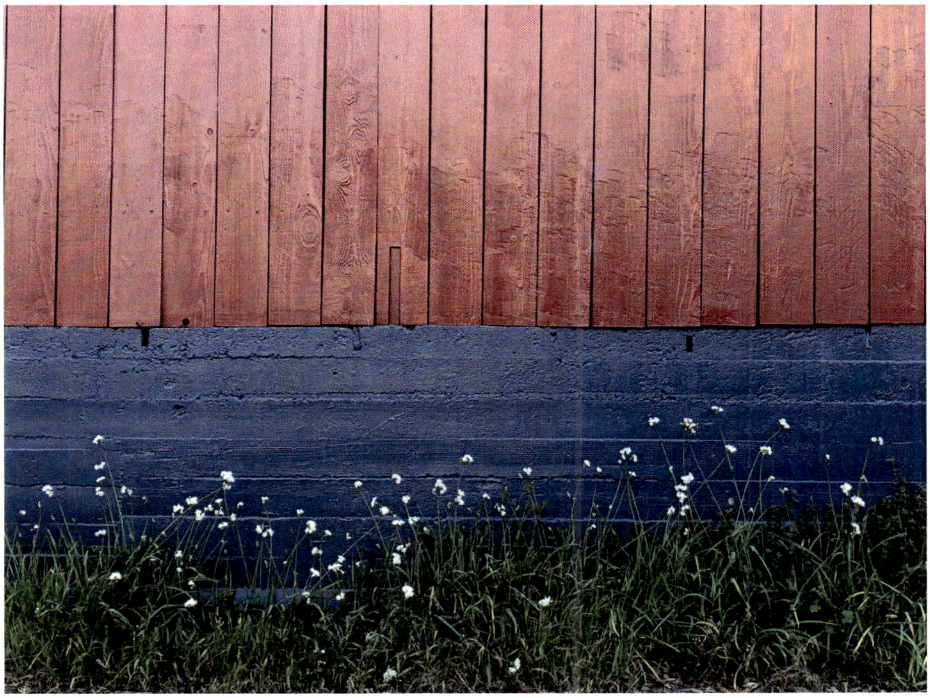

Thursday, April 23

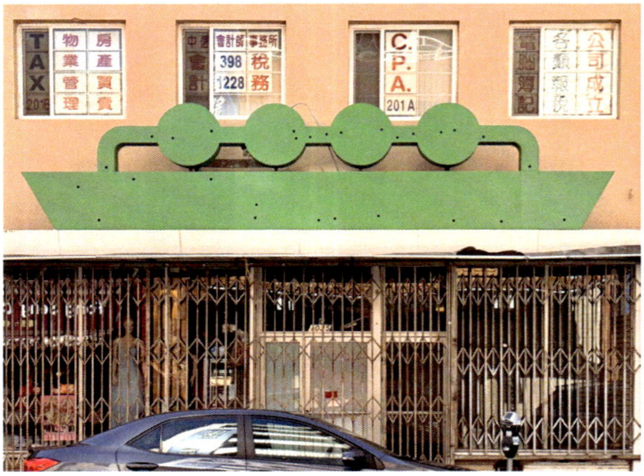
TAX
物業管理
398
1228
稅務
C.P.A.
201A
公司成立

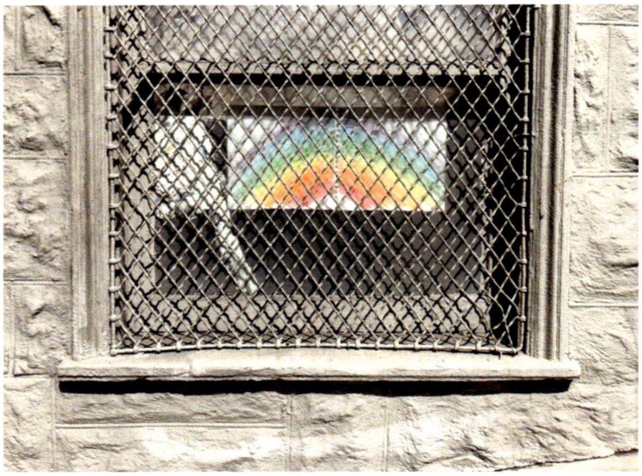

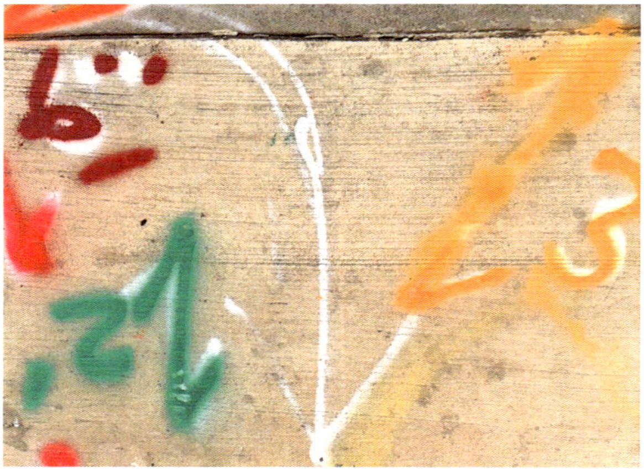

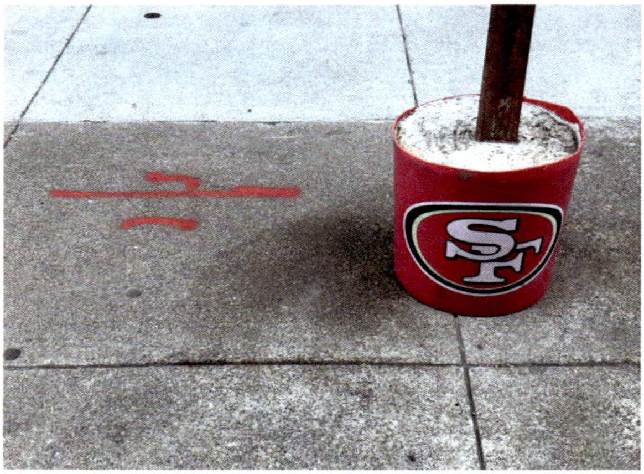
SF

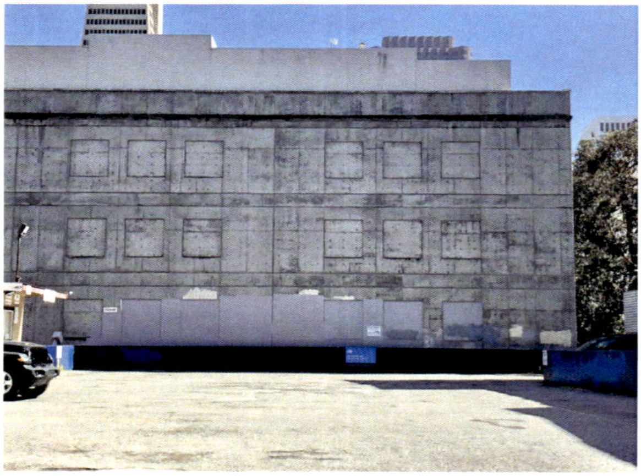

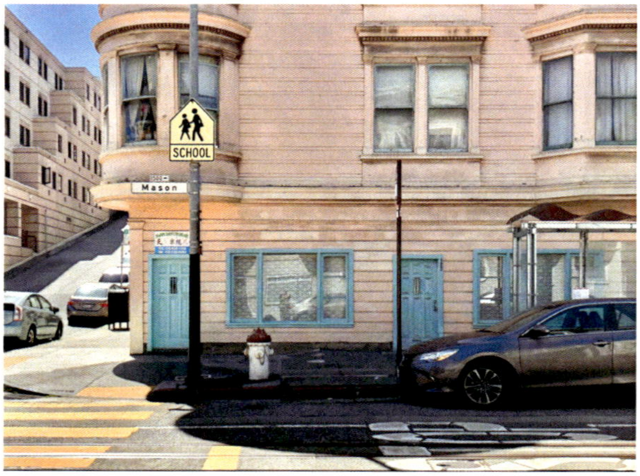
SCHOOL
Mason

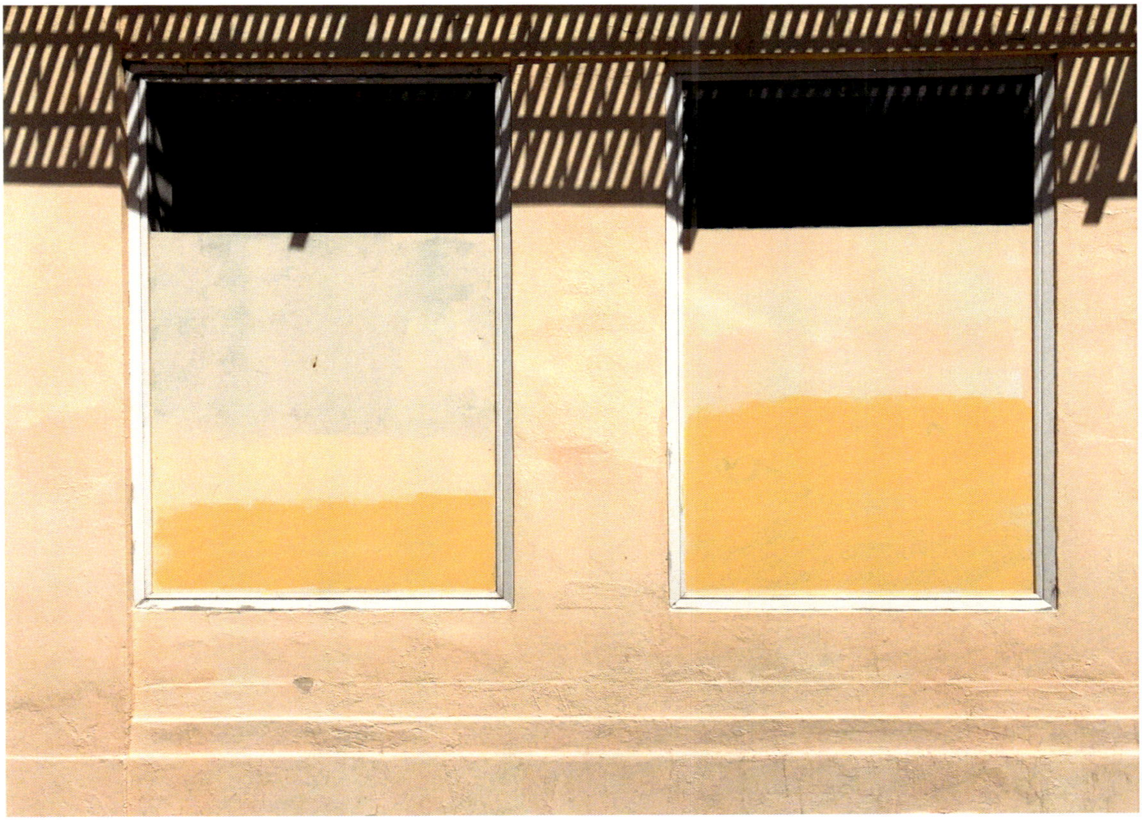

Sunday, April 26

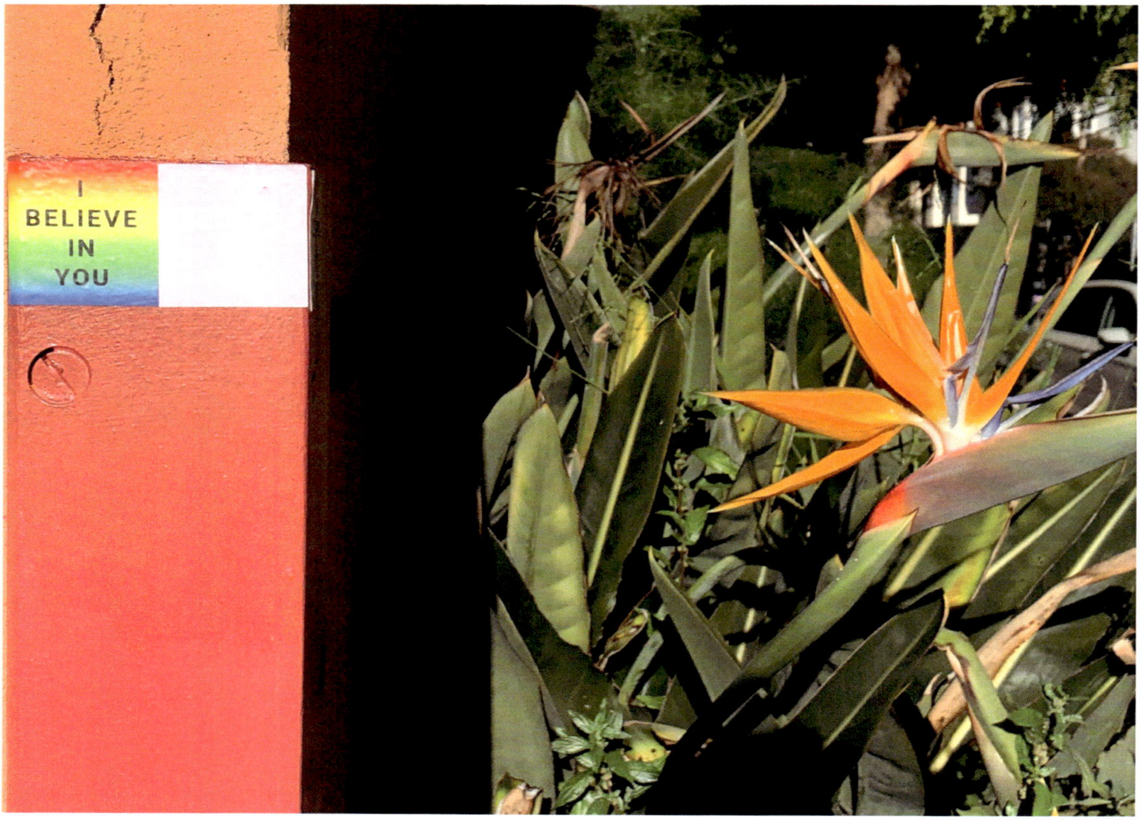
I
BELIEVE
IN
YOU

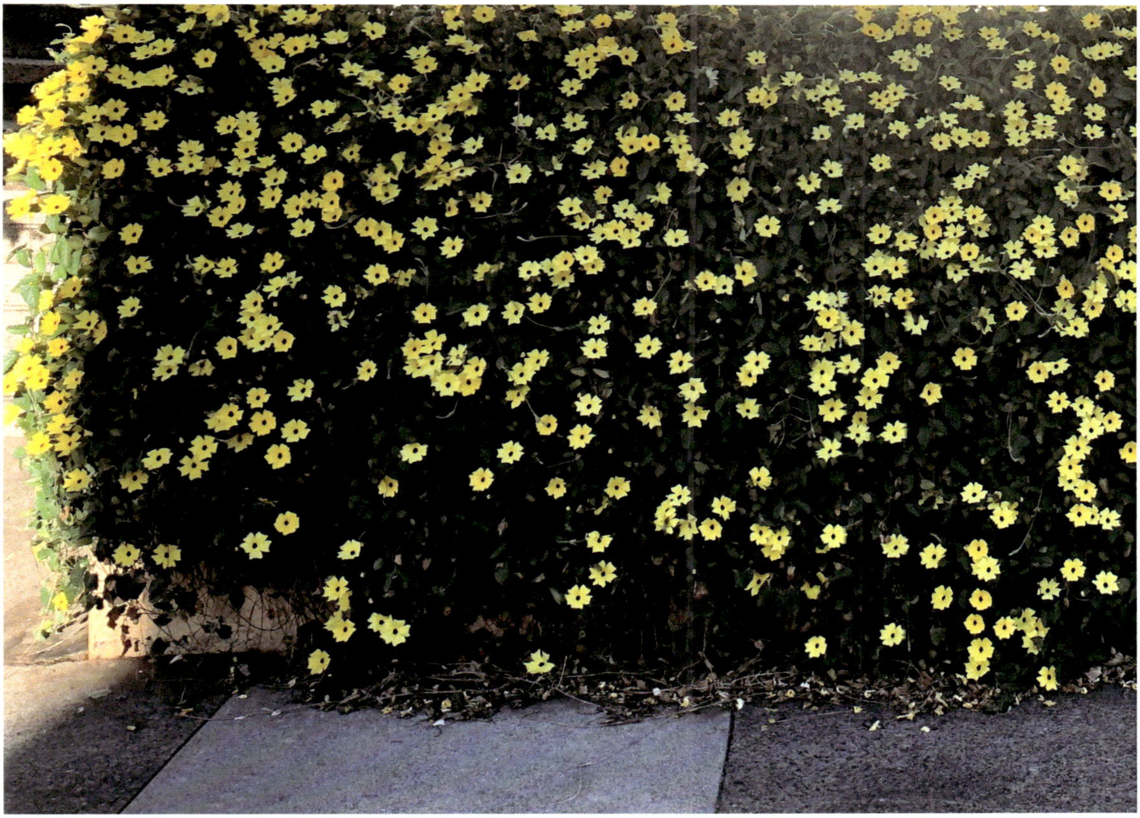

Tuesday, April 28

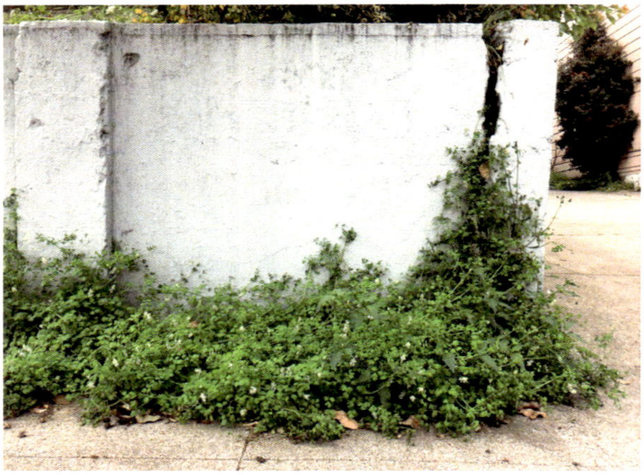

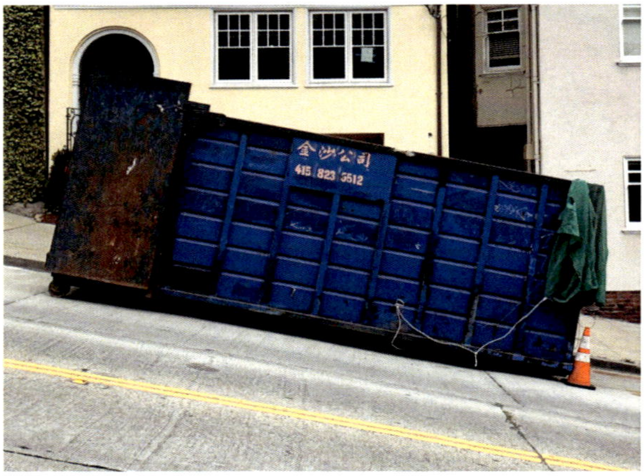
金沙公司
415 823 5512

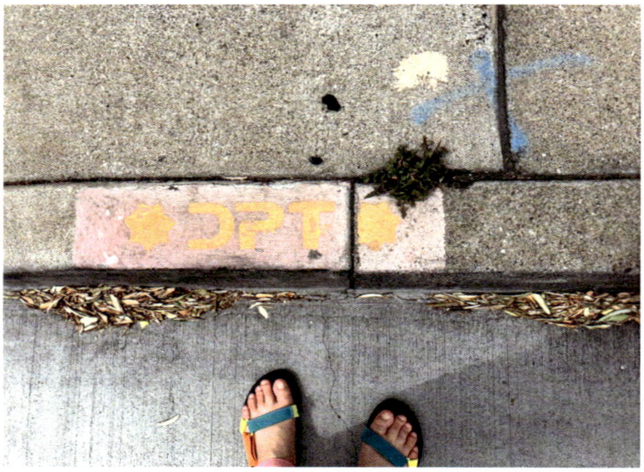
DPT

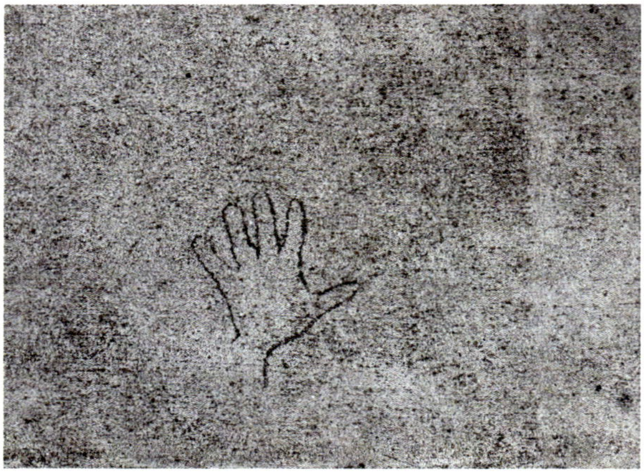

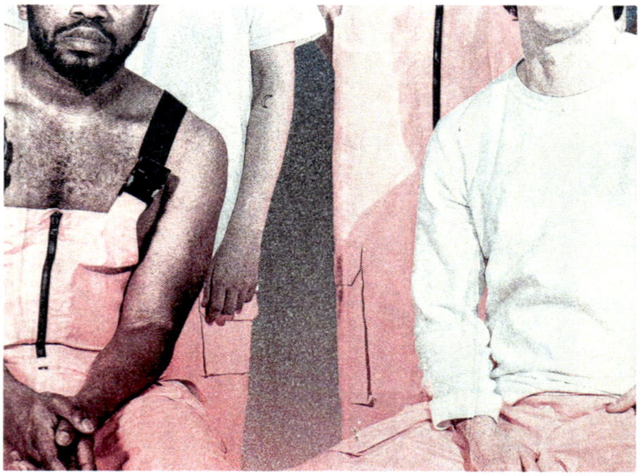

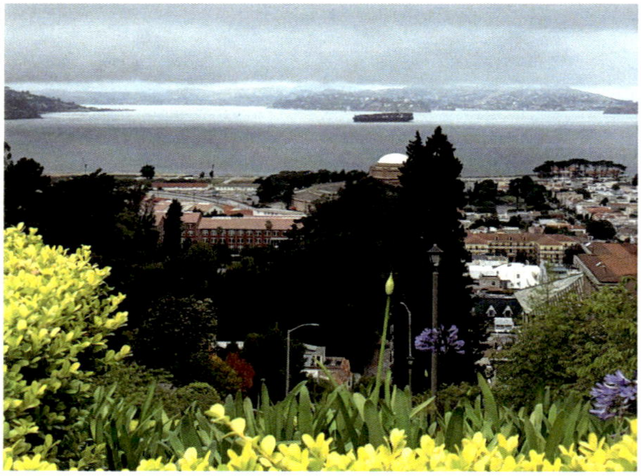

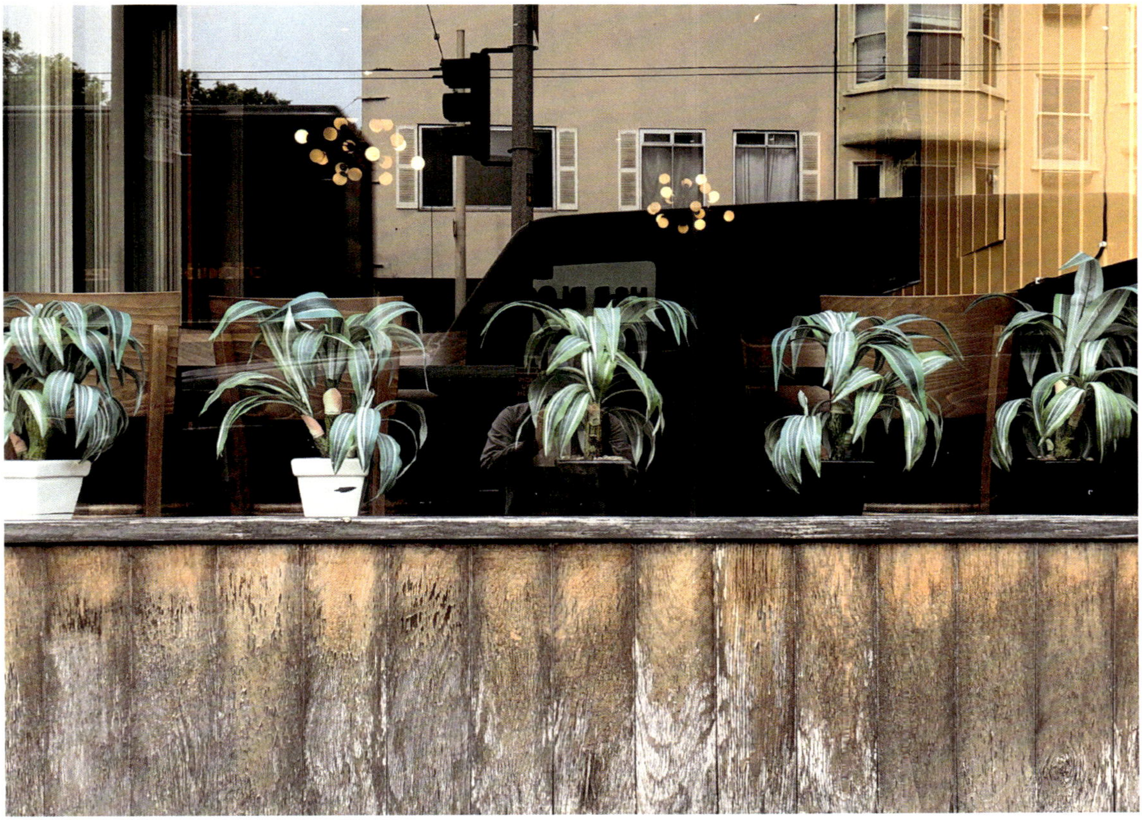

Saturday, May 2

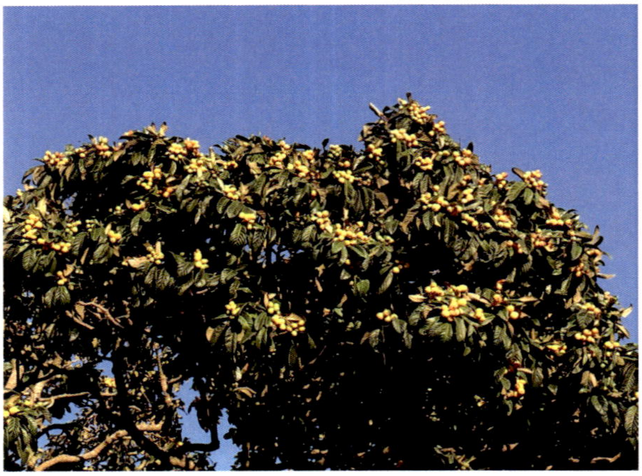
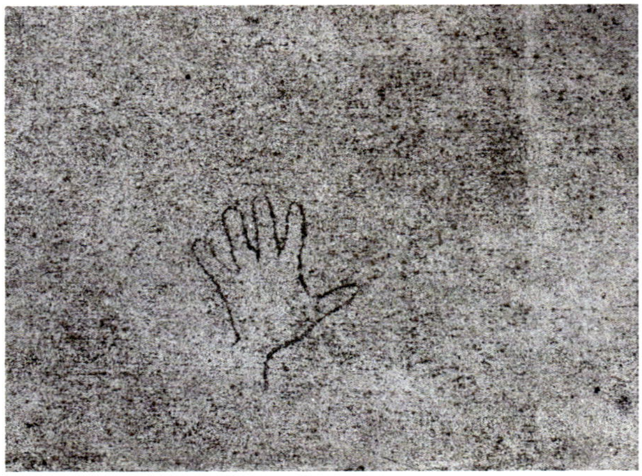
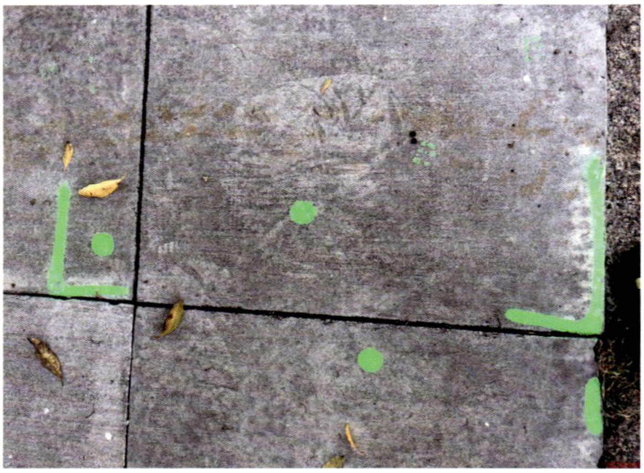
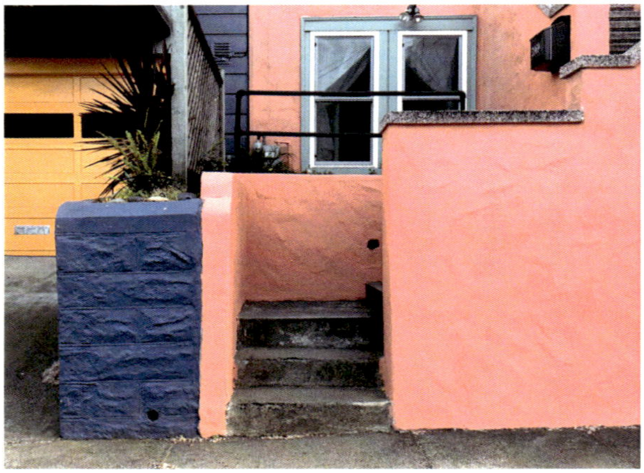
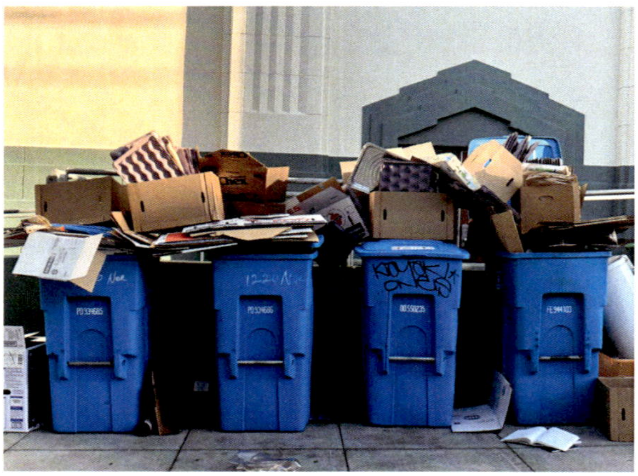
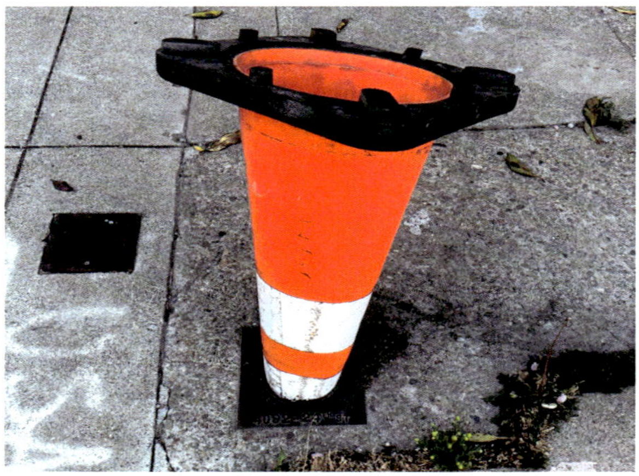

Sunday, May 3

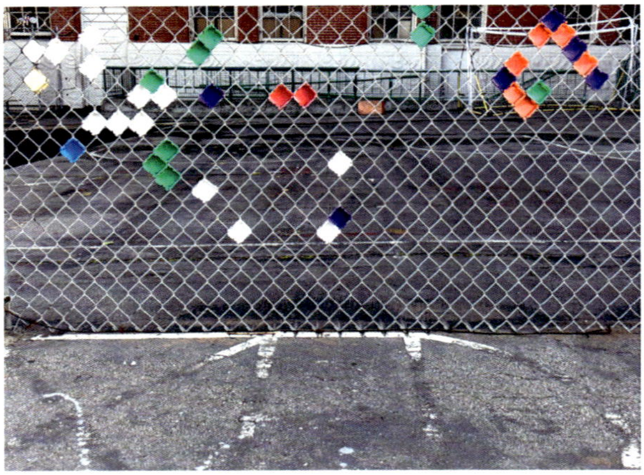

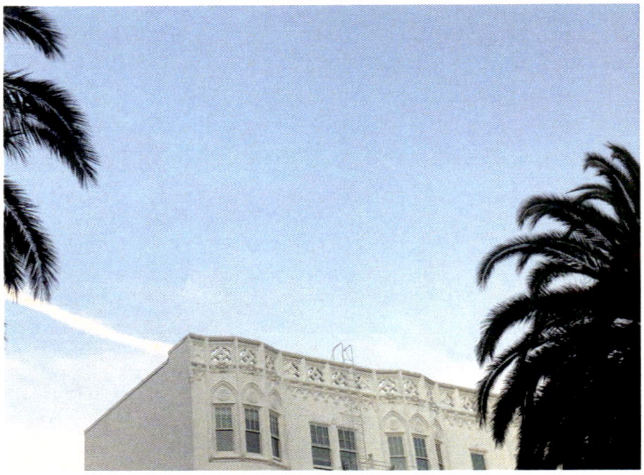

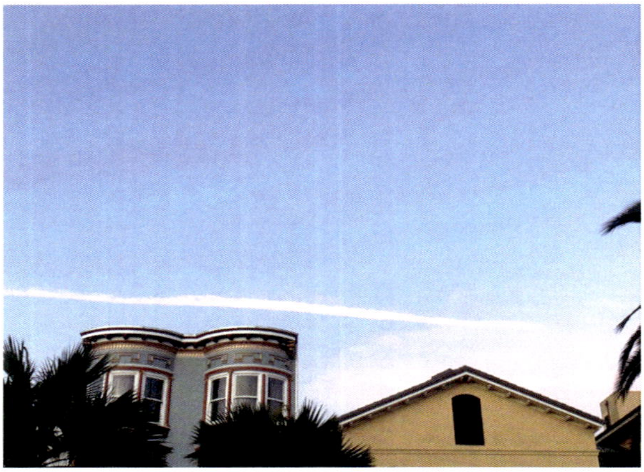

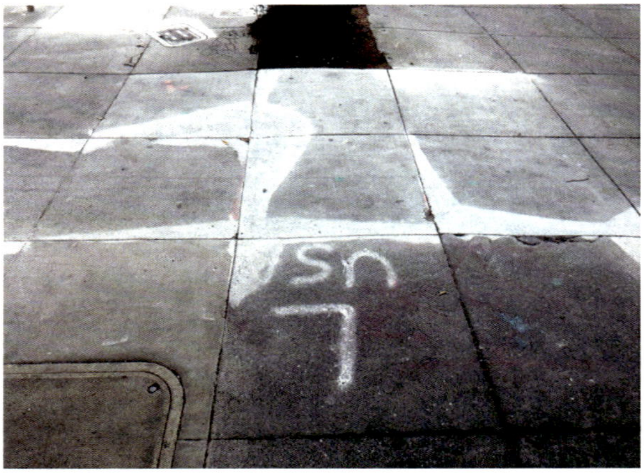

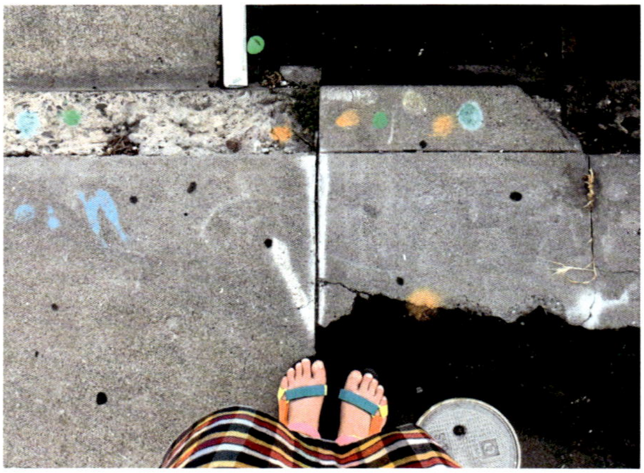

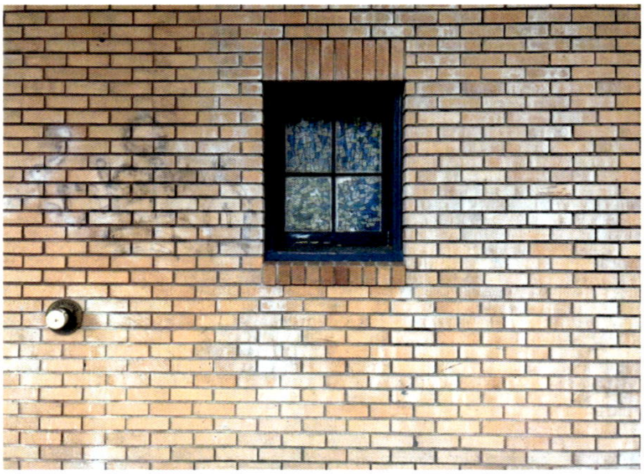

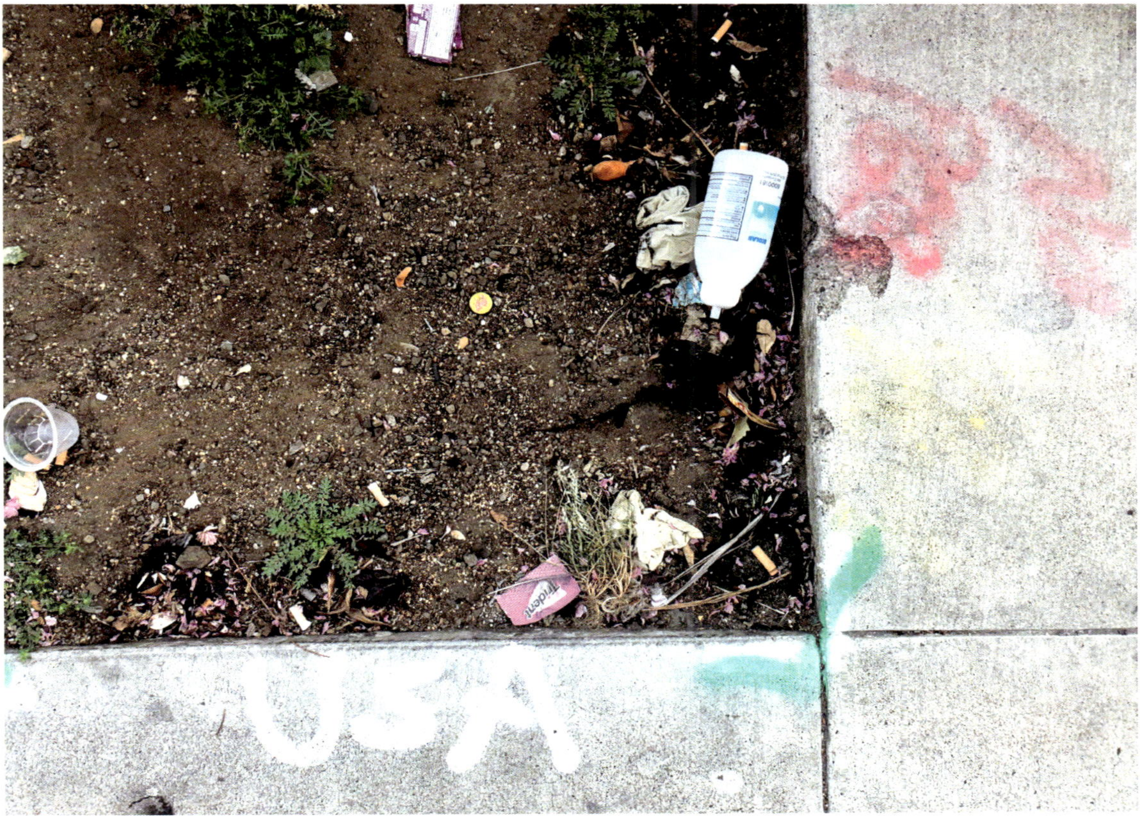

Thursday, May 7

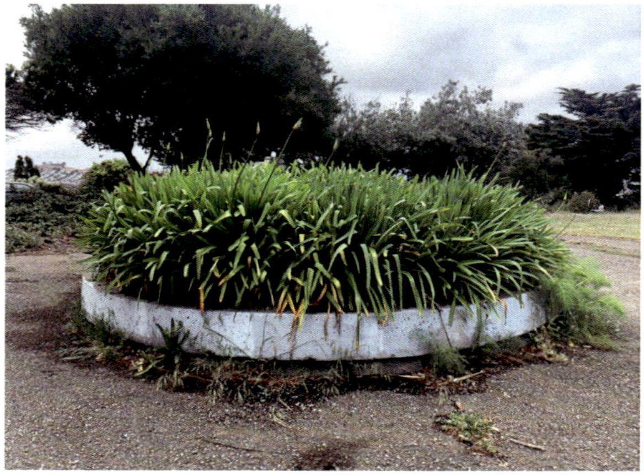

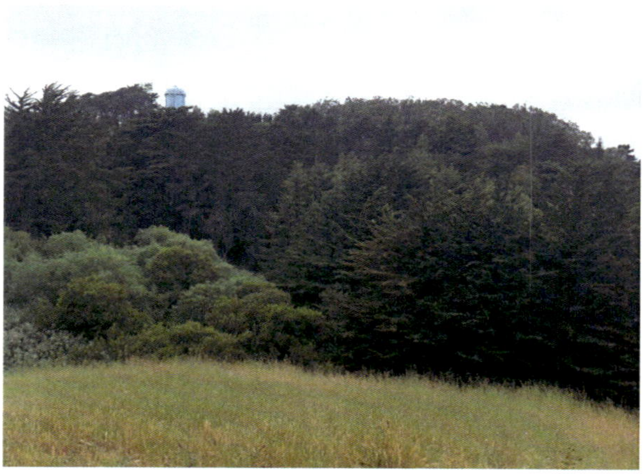

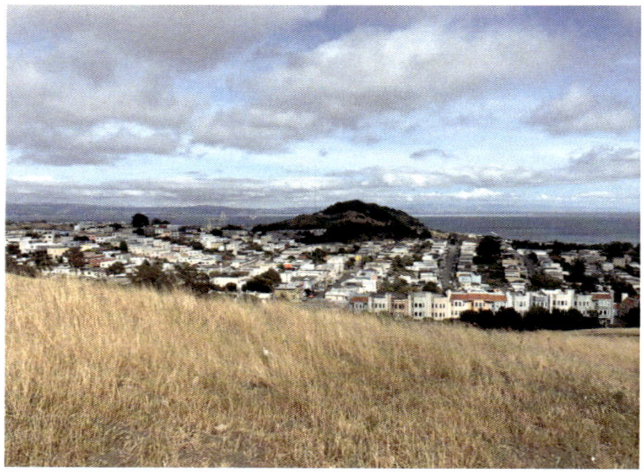

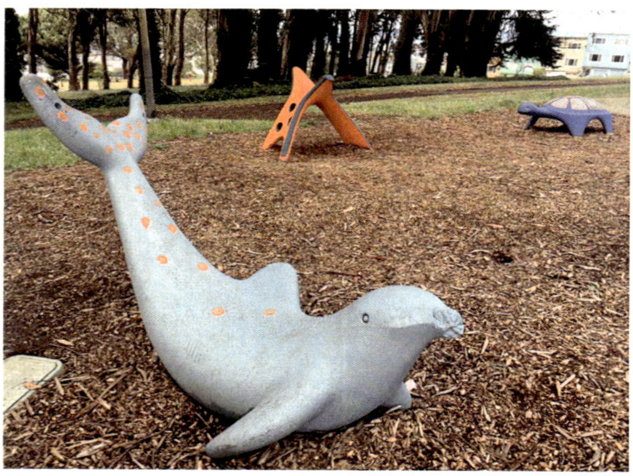

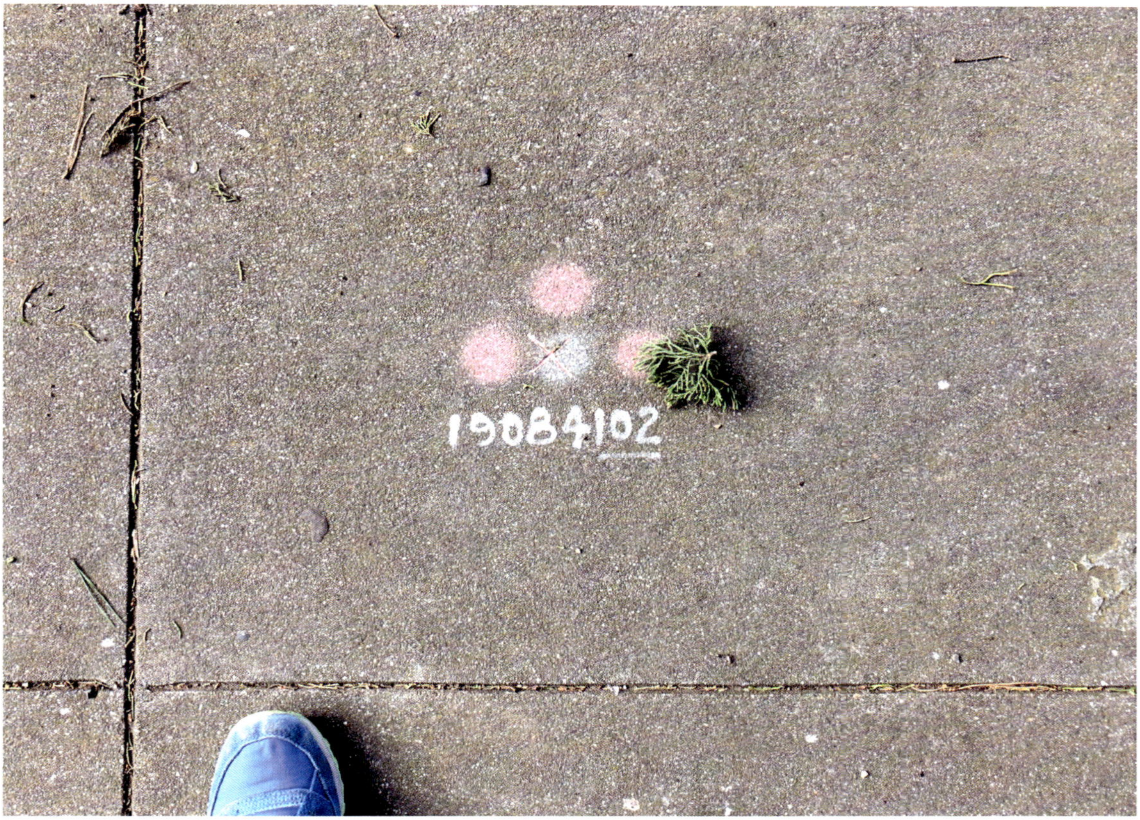

Thursday, May 14

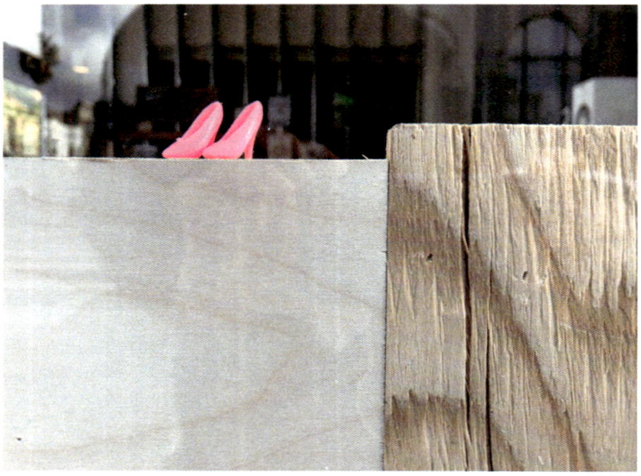

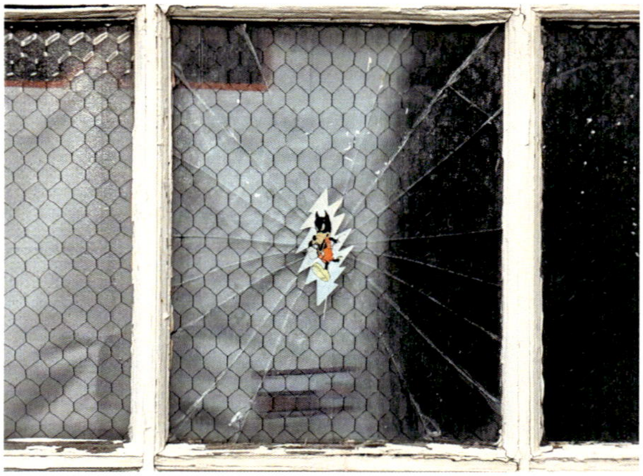

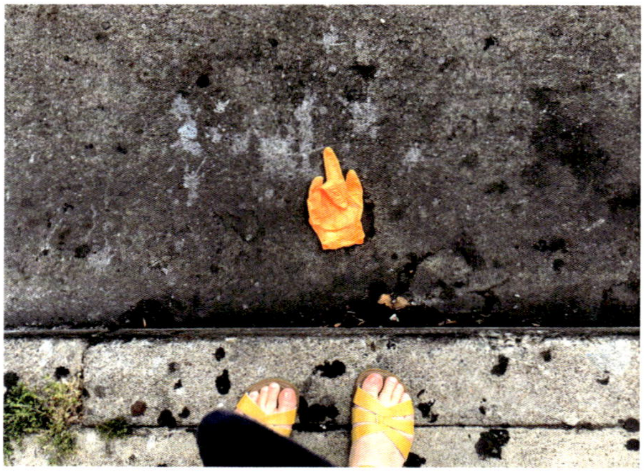

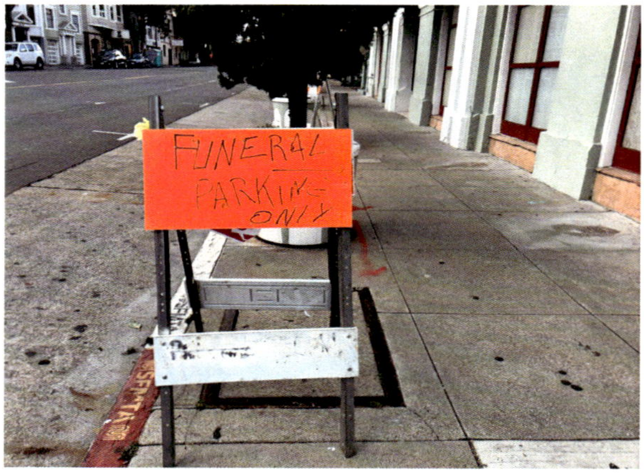
FUNERAL
PARKING
ONLY

PETCO
DR. FAUCI for PRESIDENT

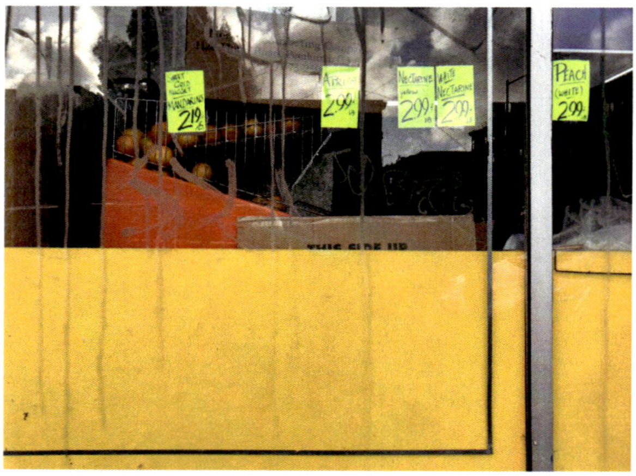

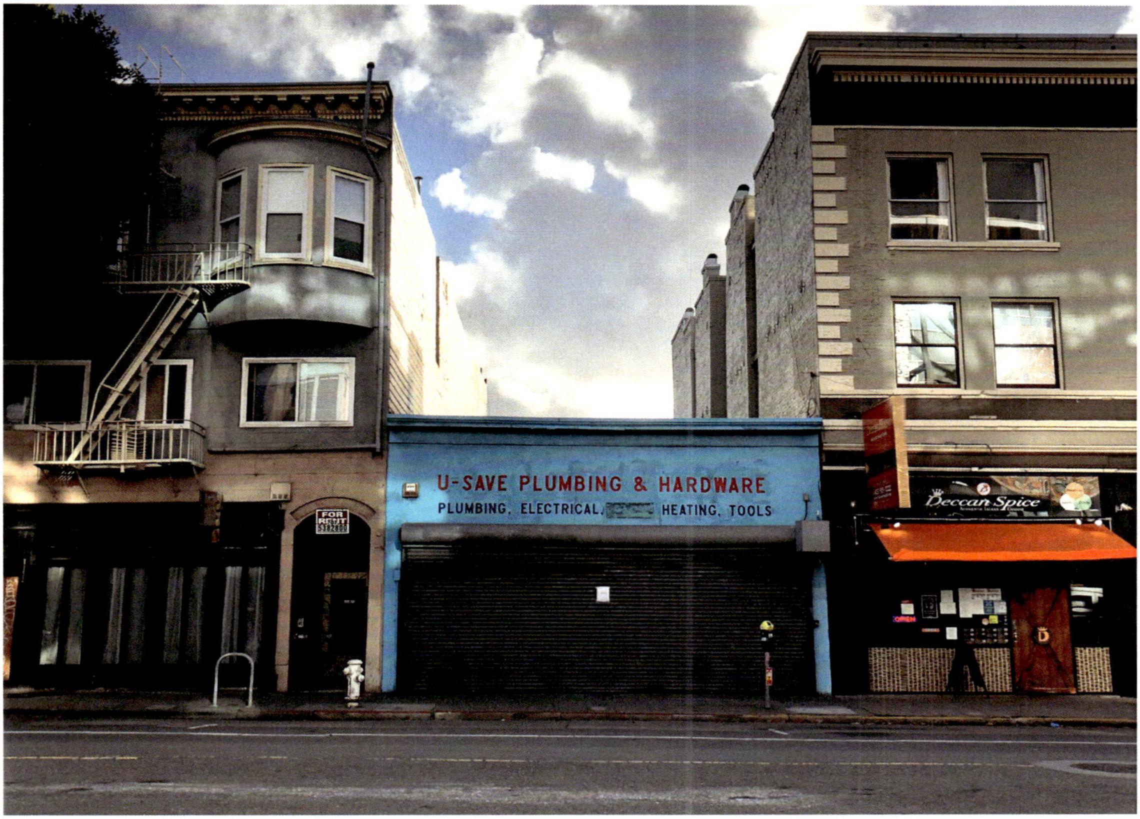

Monday, May 18

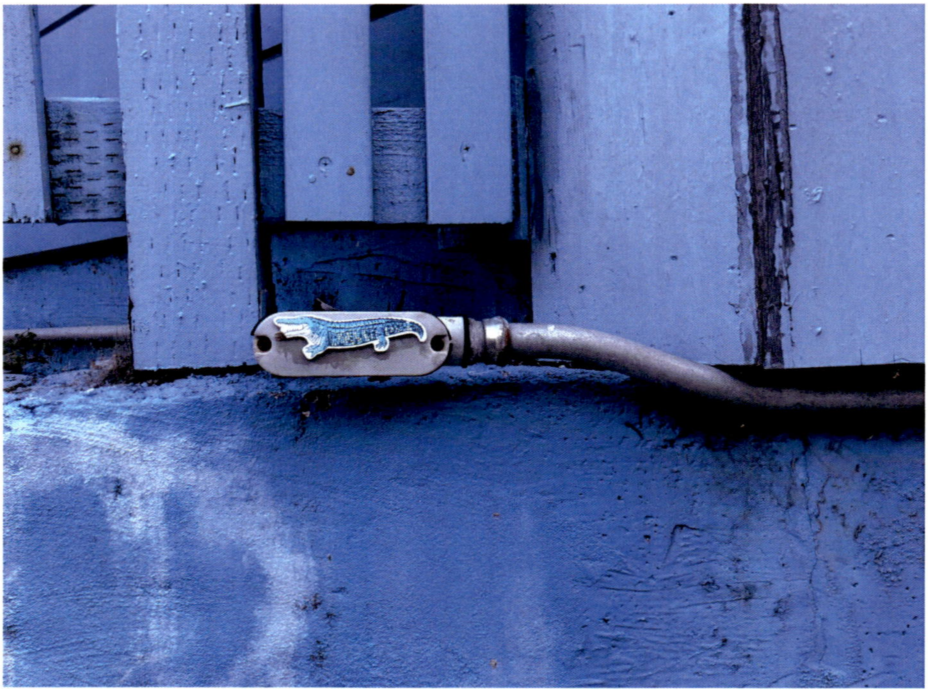

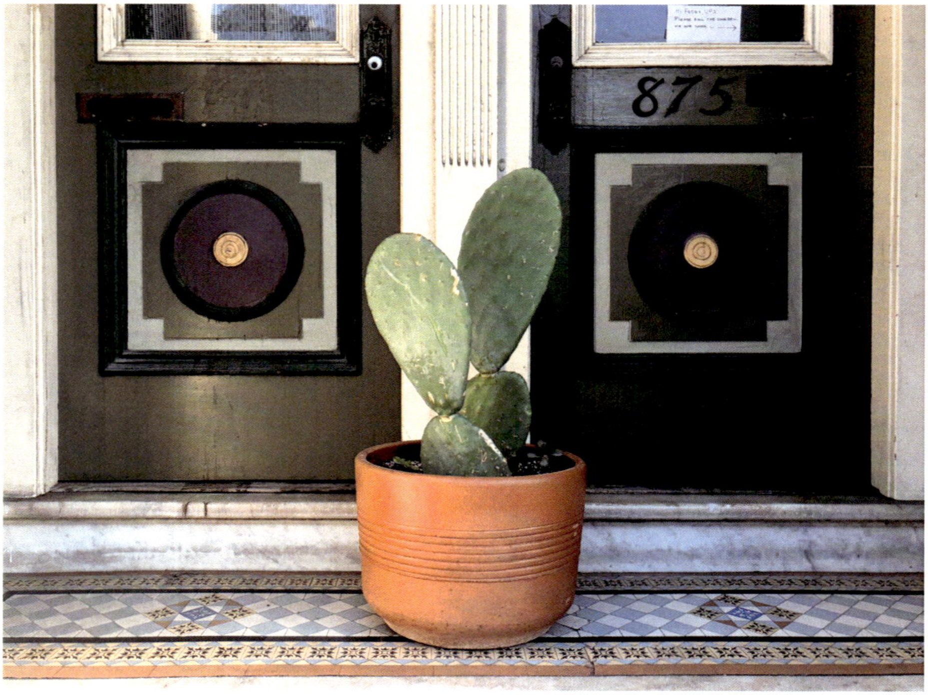
875

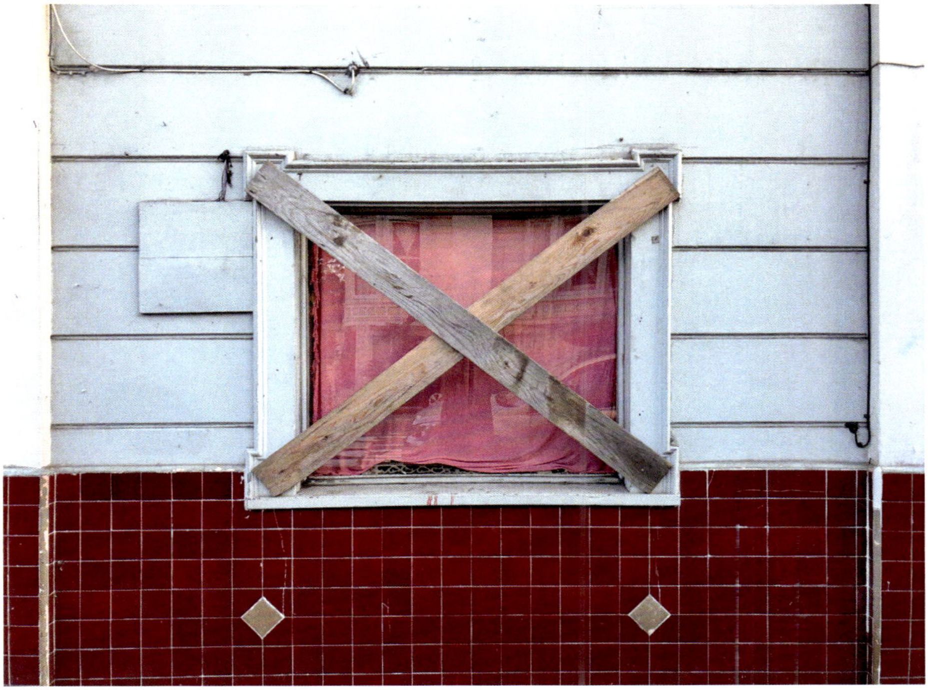

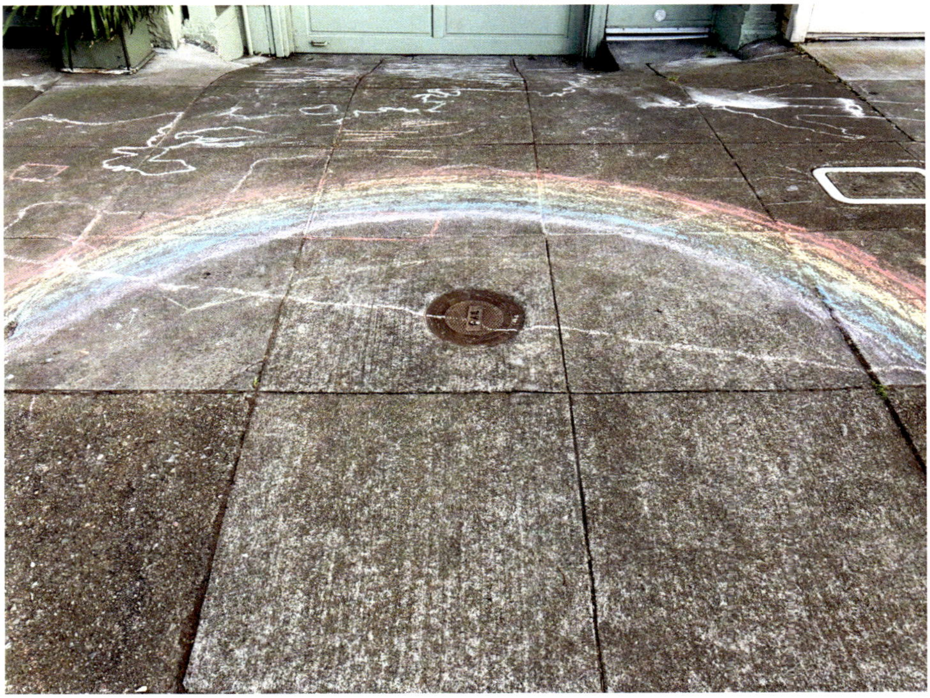

Thursday, May 21

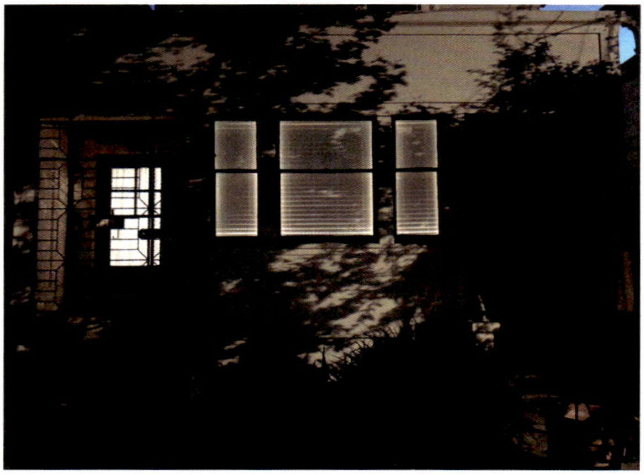

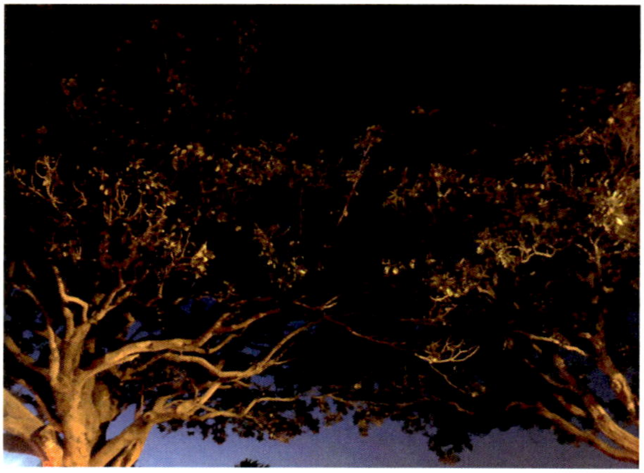

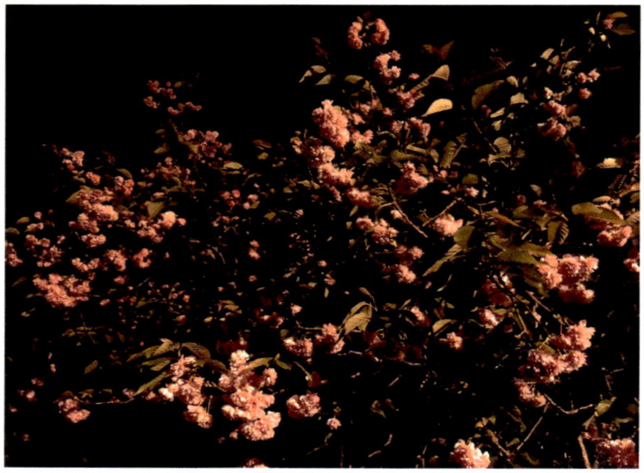

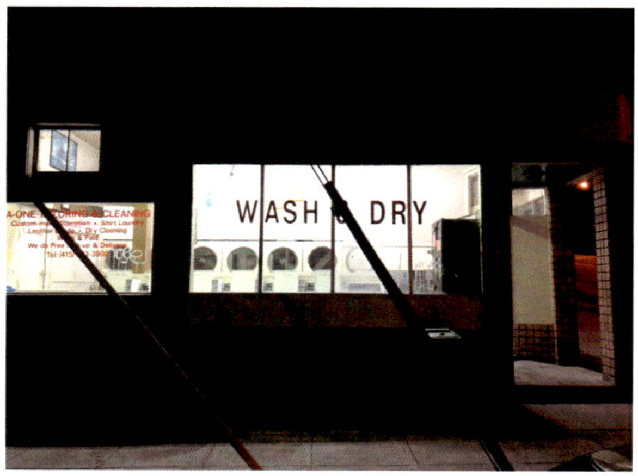
WASH
DRY

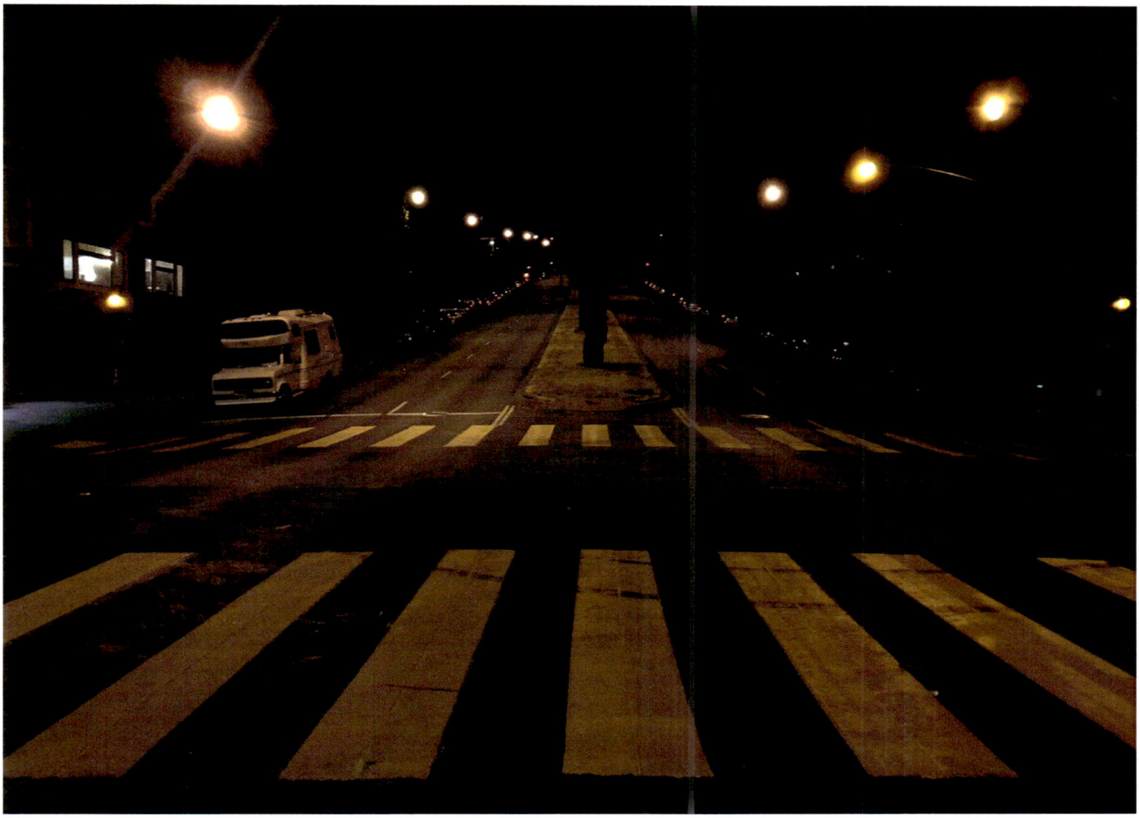

Friday, May 22

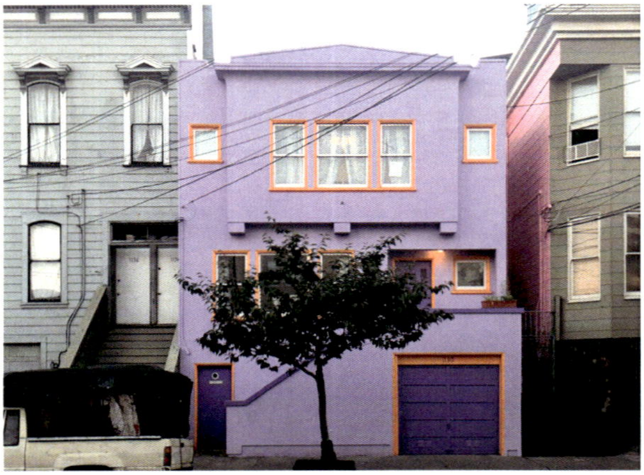

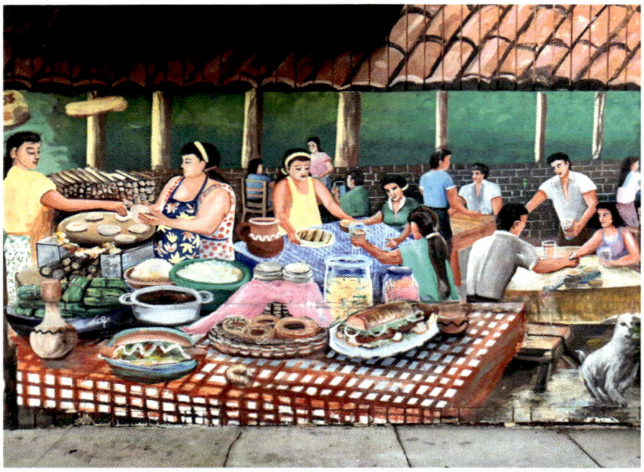

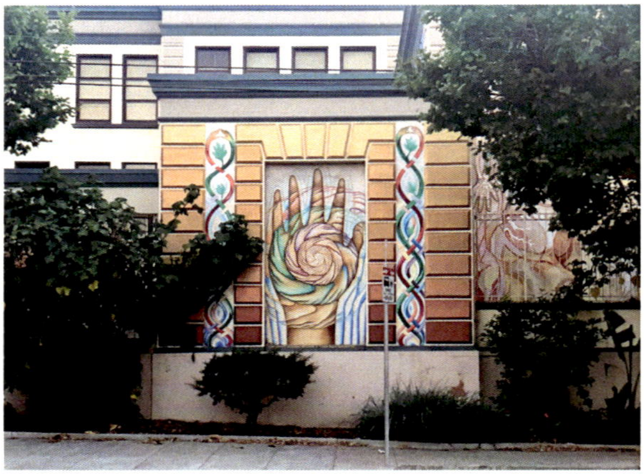

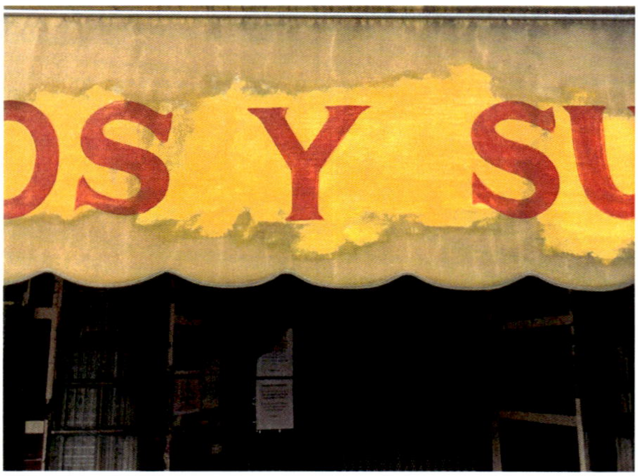
OS Y SU

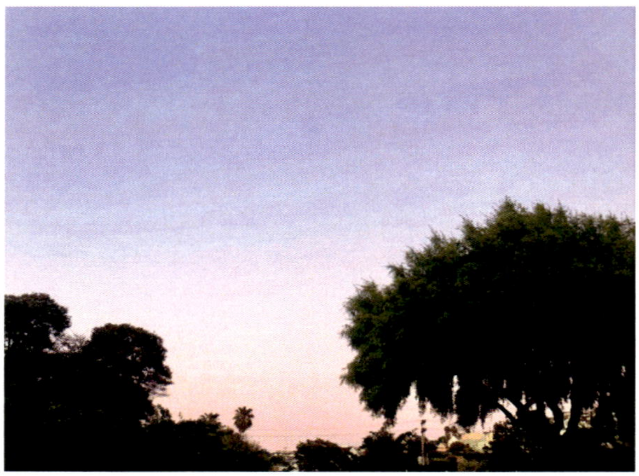

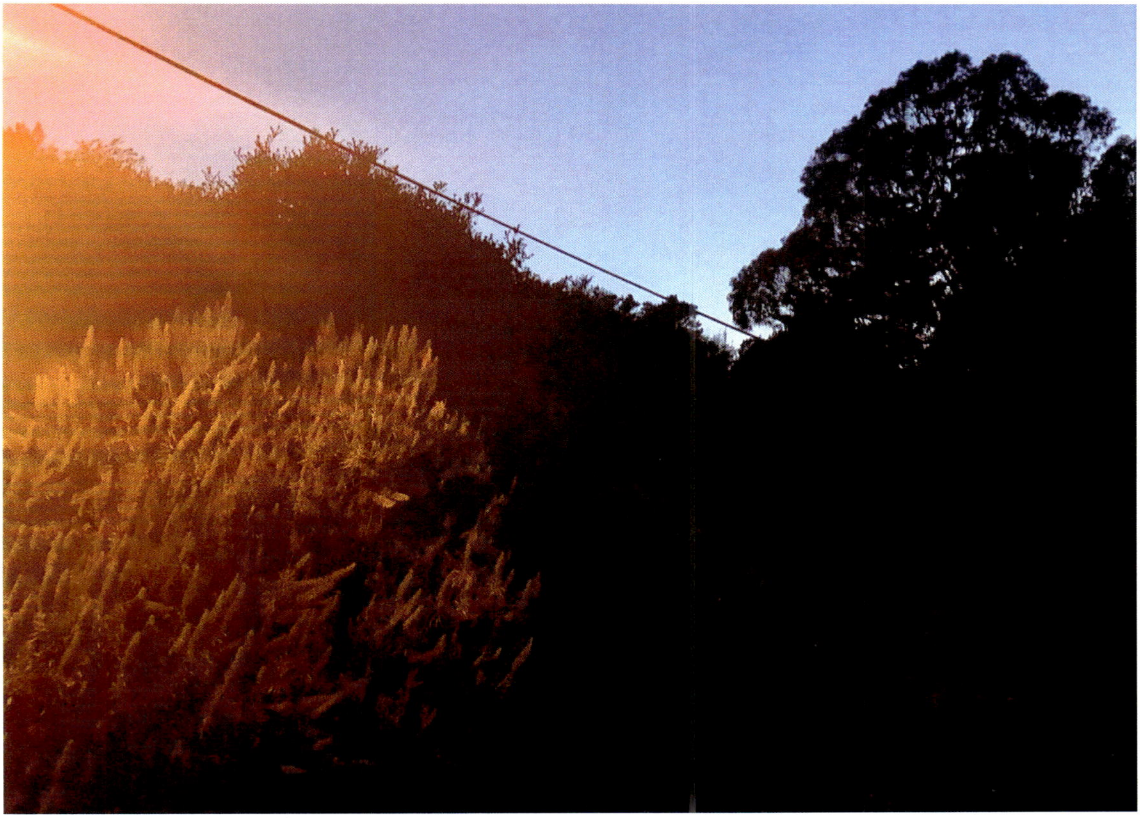

Sunday, May 24

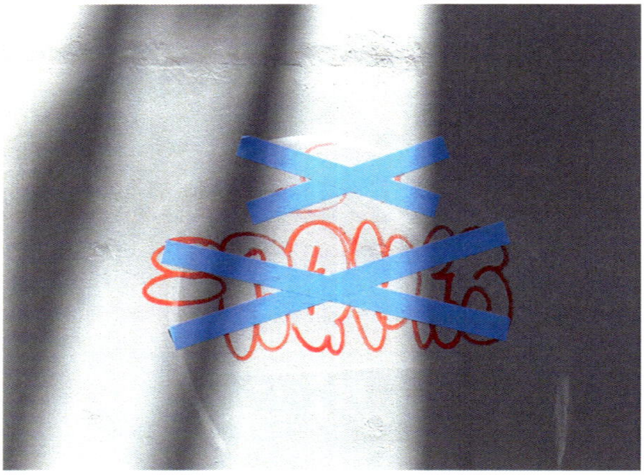

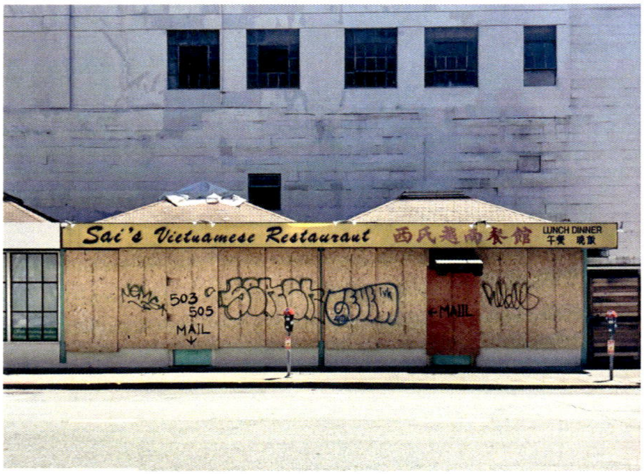
Sai's Vietnamese Restaurant
LUNCH DINNER
503
505
MAIL

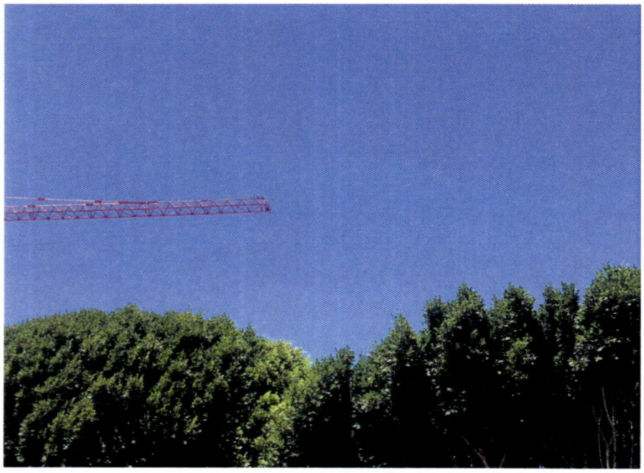

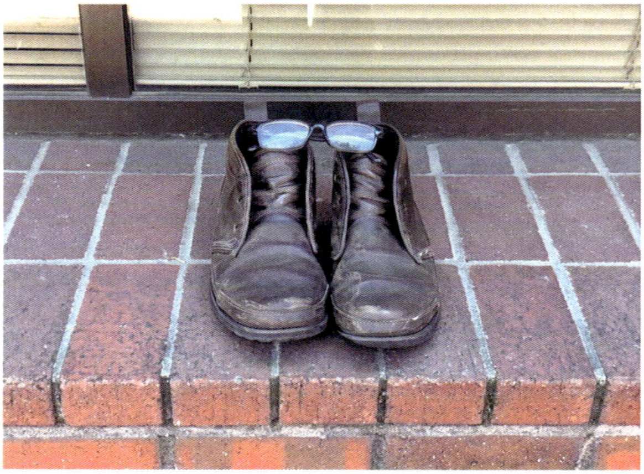

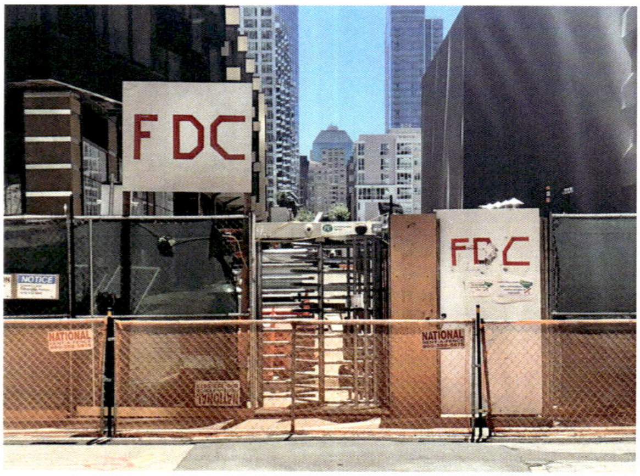
FDC
FDC
NOTICE
NATIONAL

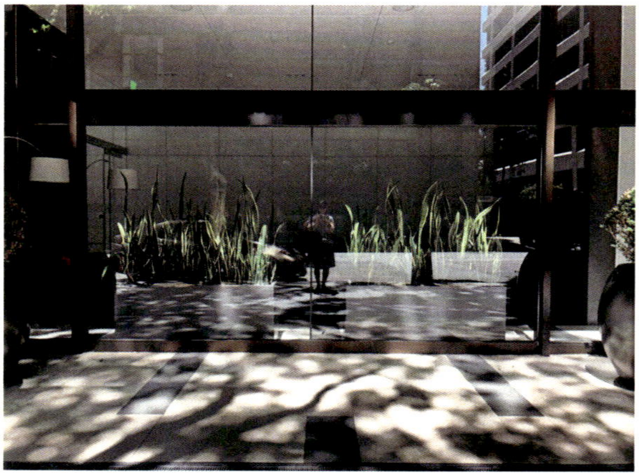

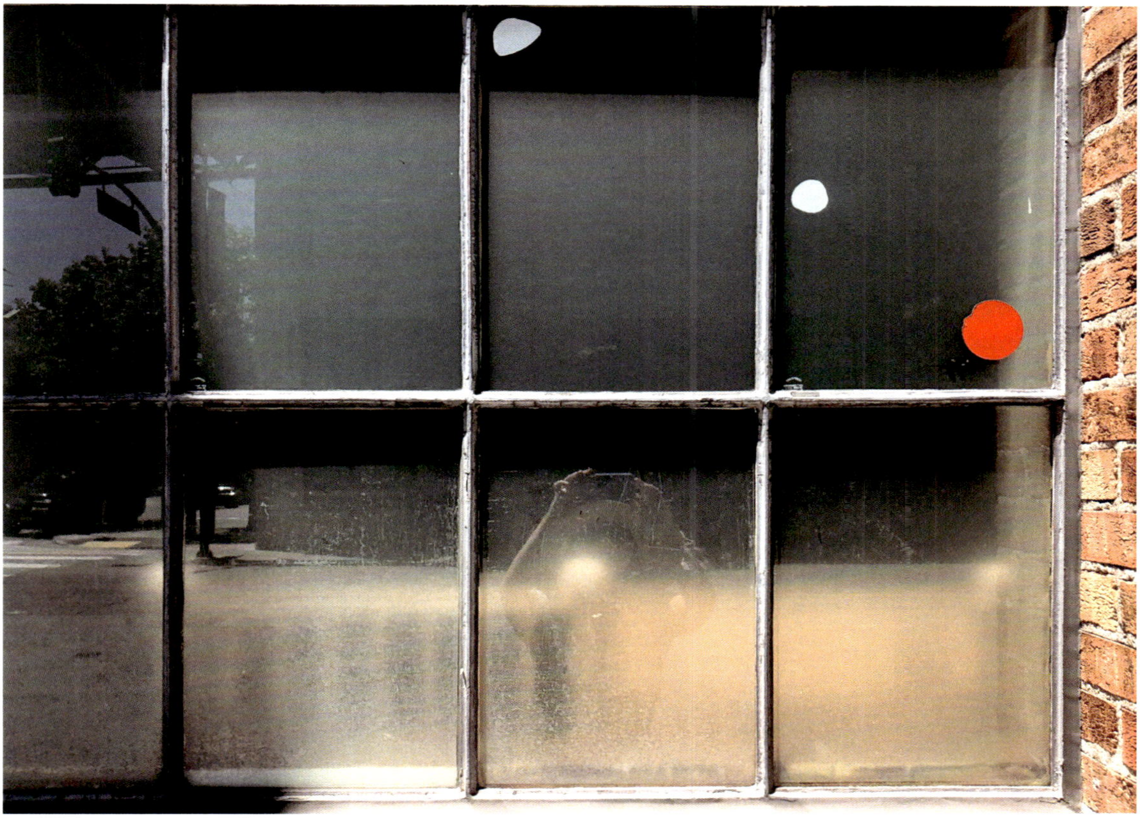

Monday, May 25

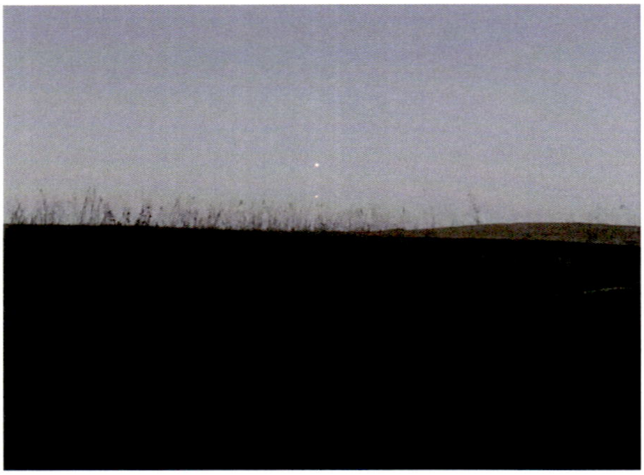
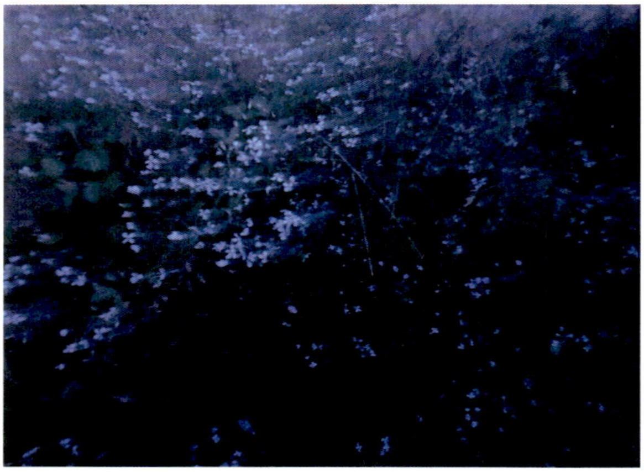
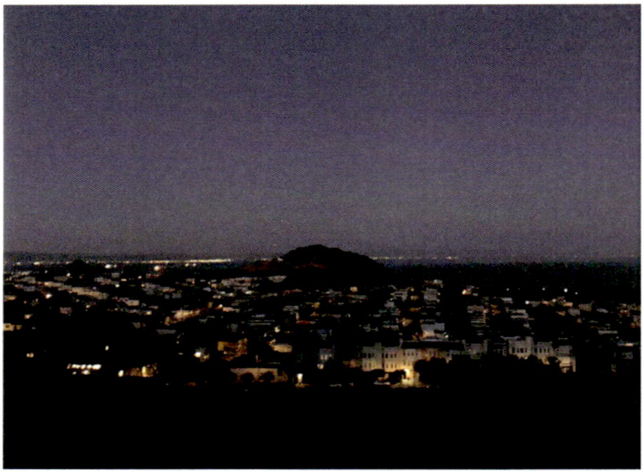
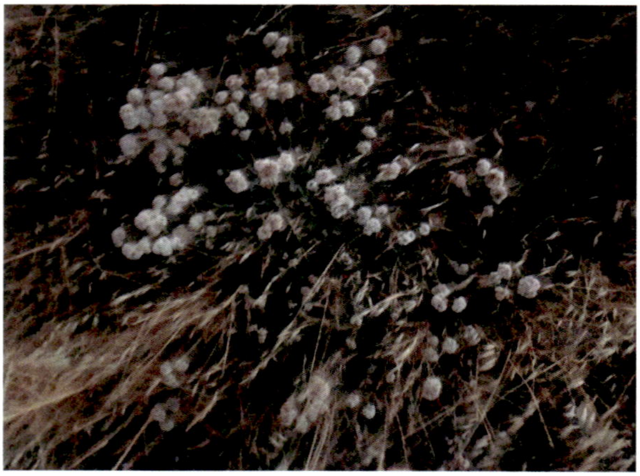
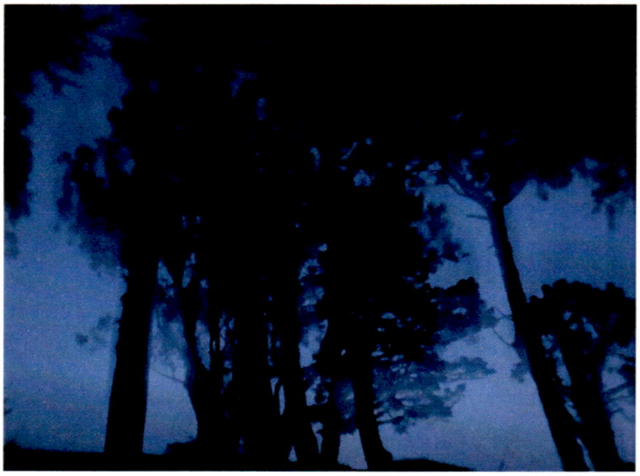

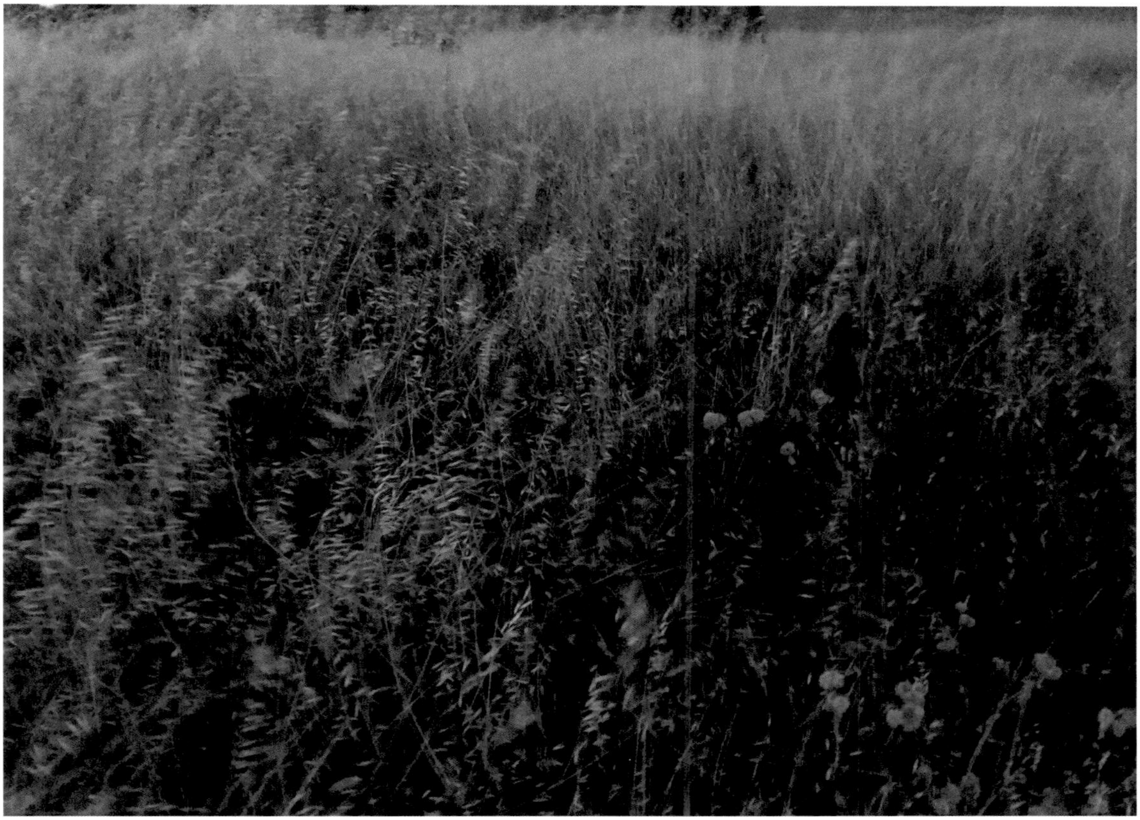

Tuesday, May 26

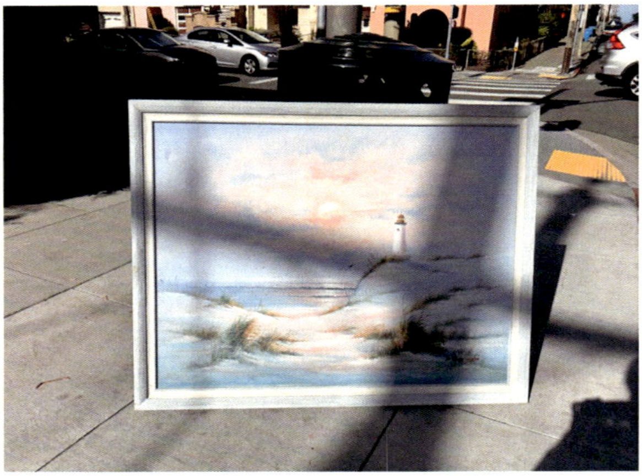

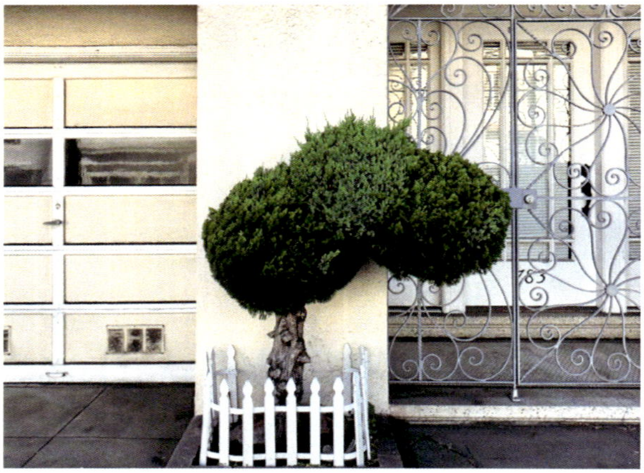

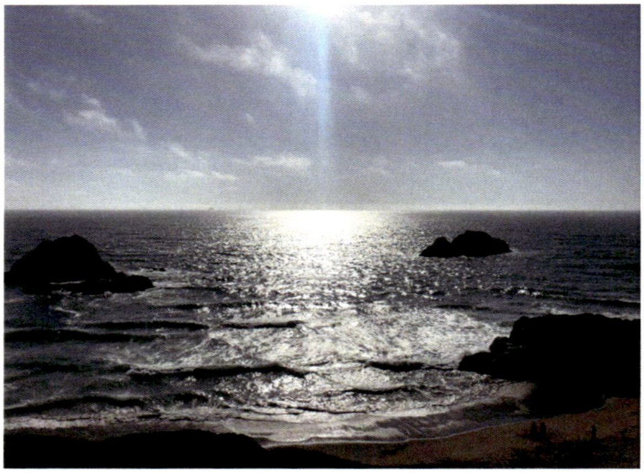

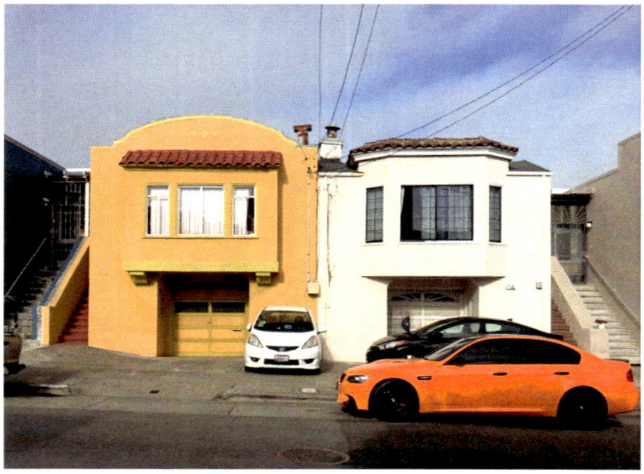

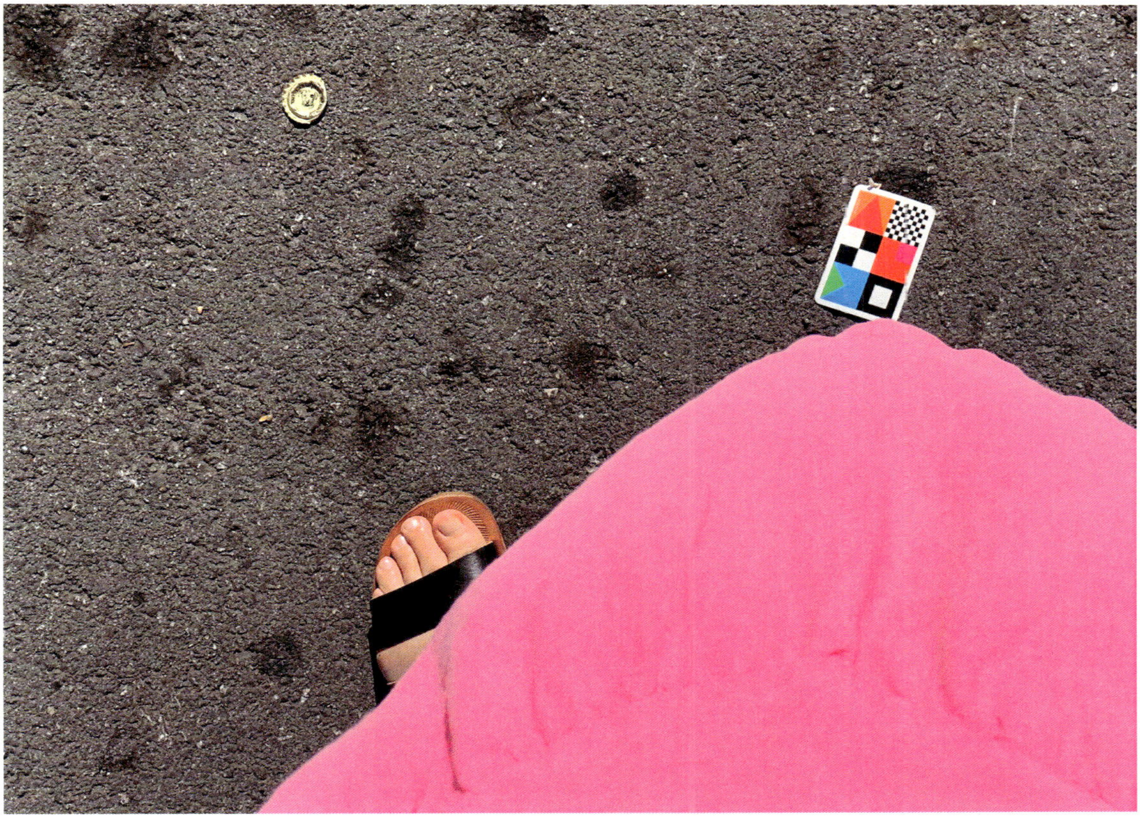

Wednesday, May 27

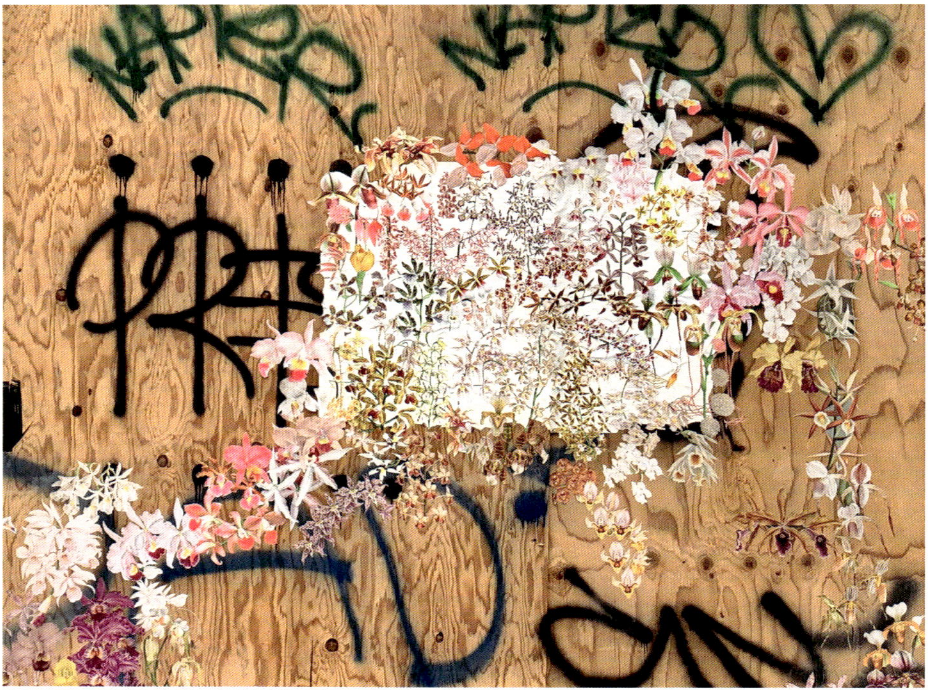

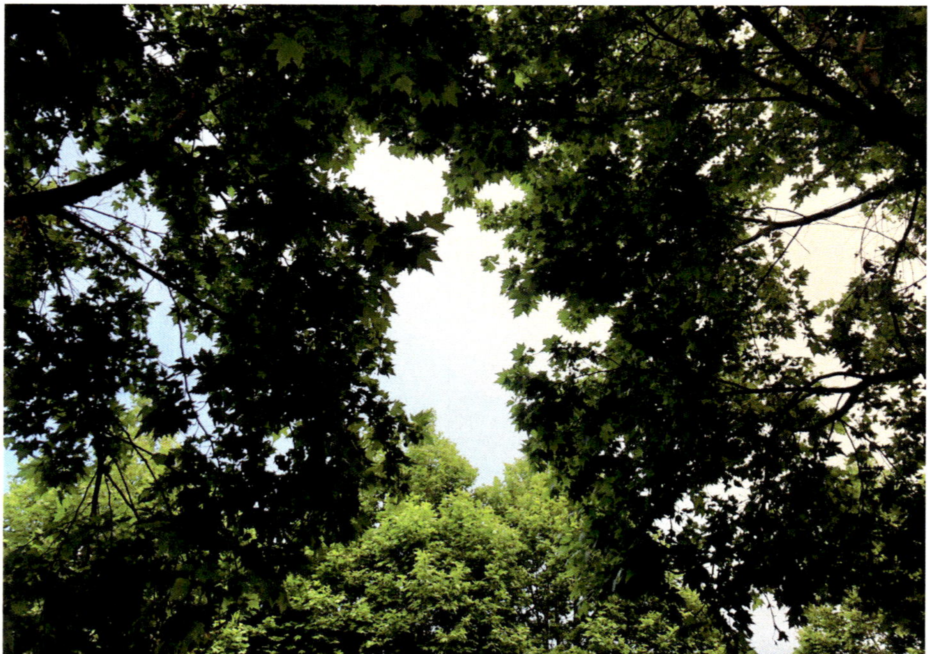

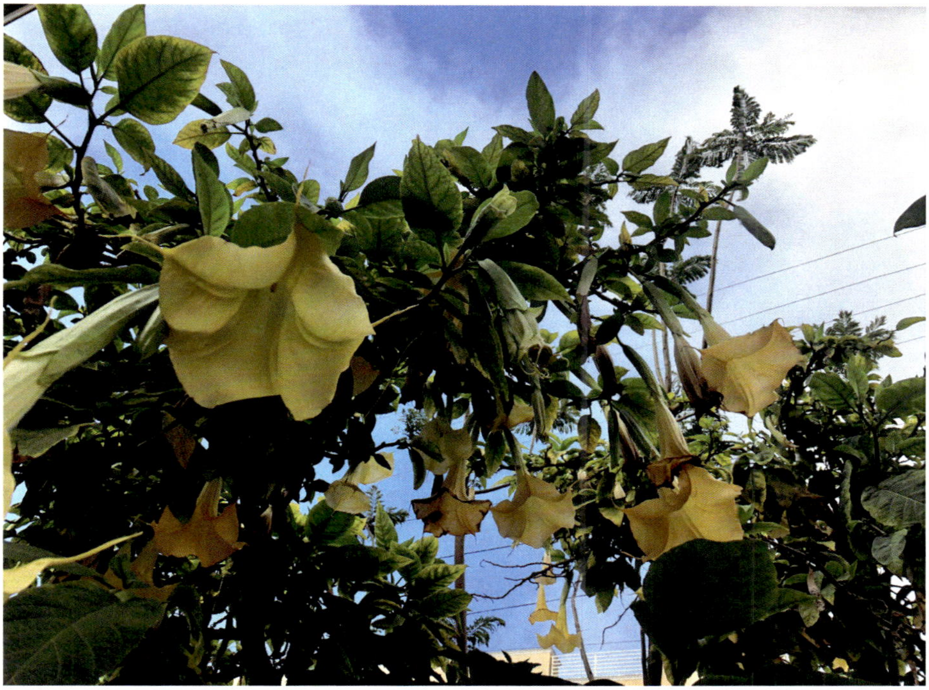

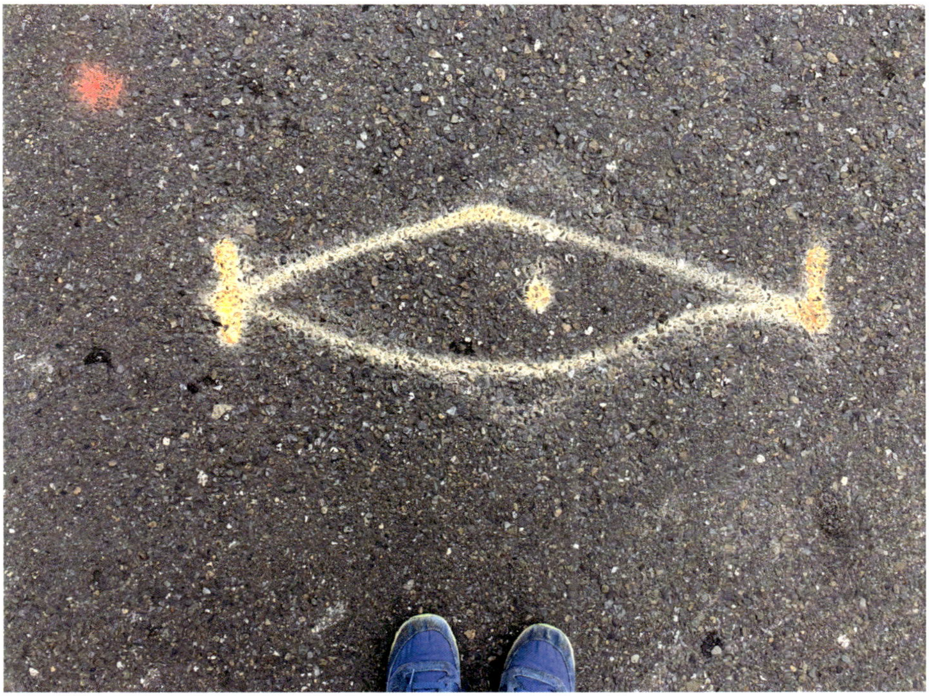

Thursday, May 28

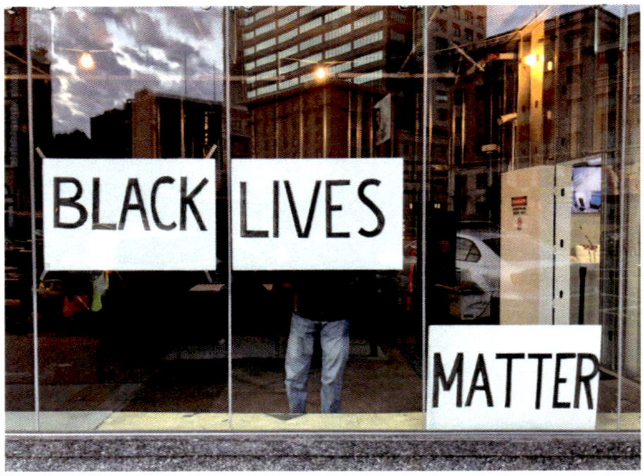
BLACK
LIVES
MATTER

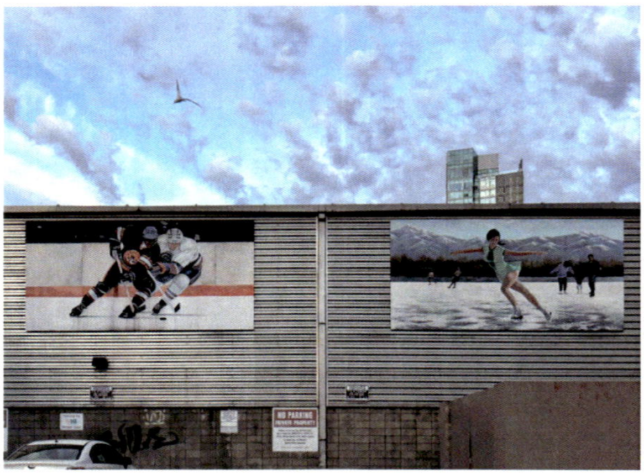

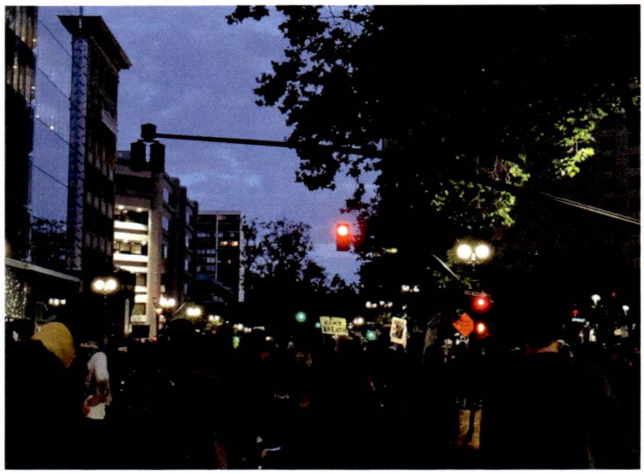

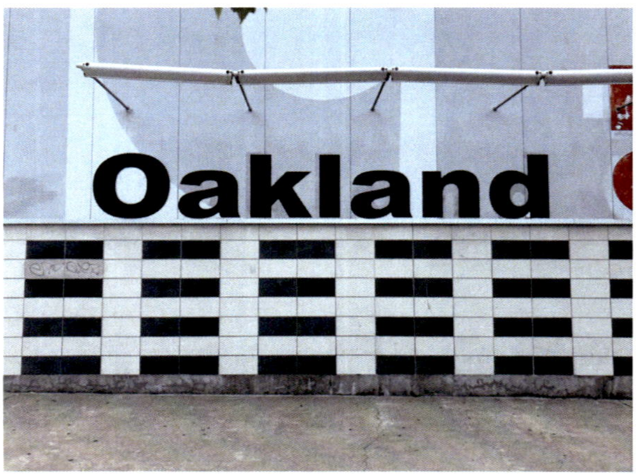
Oakland

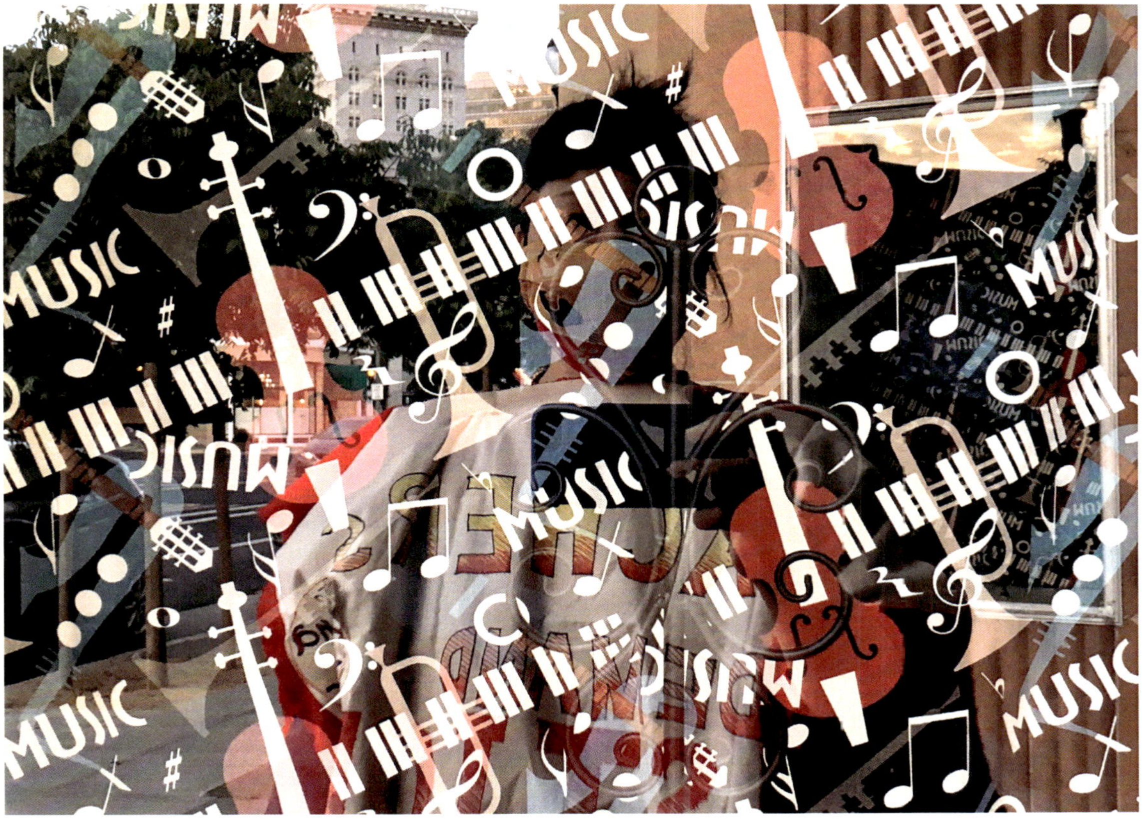

Friday, May 29

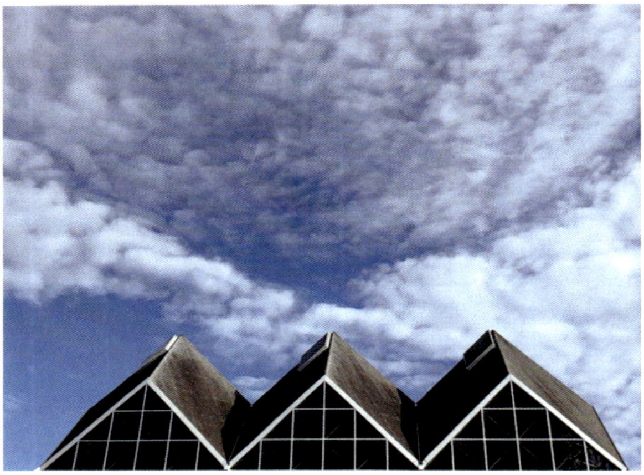

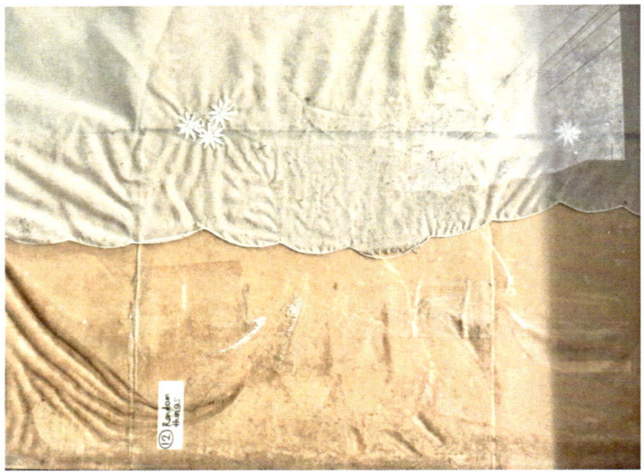

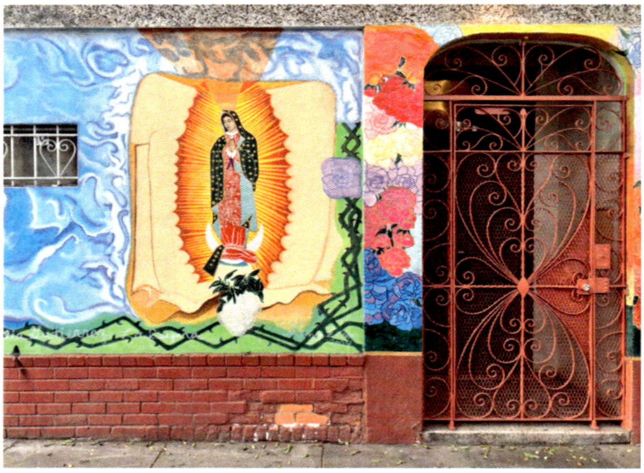

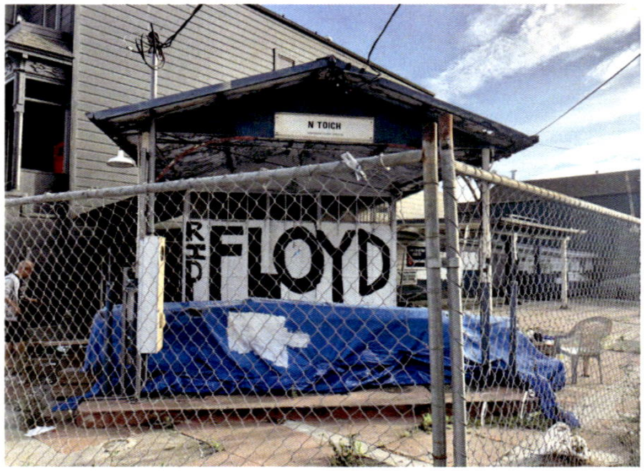
N'TOICH
FLOYD

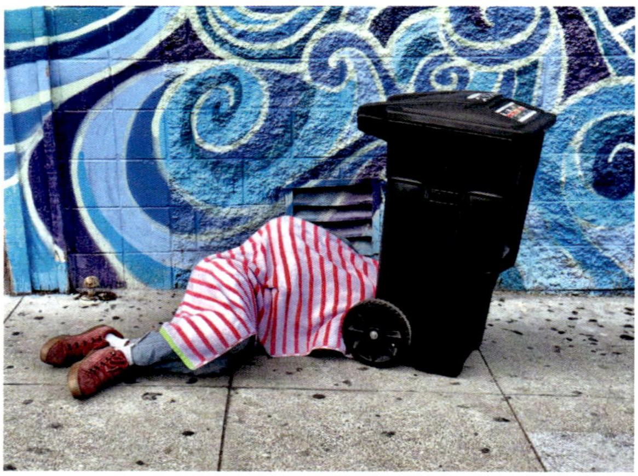

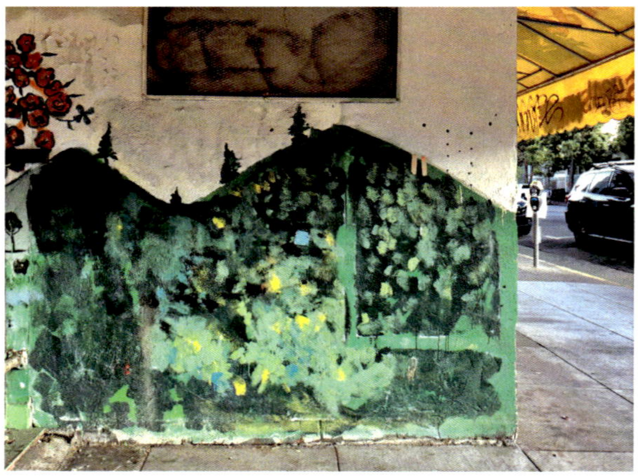

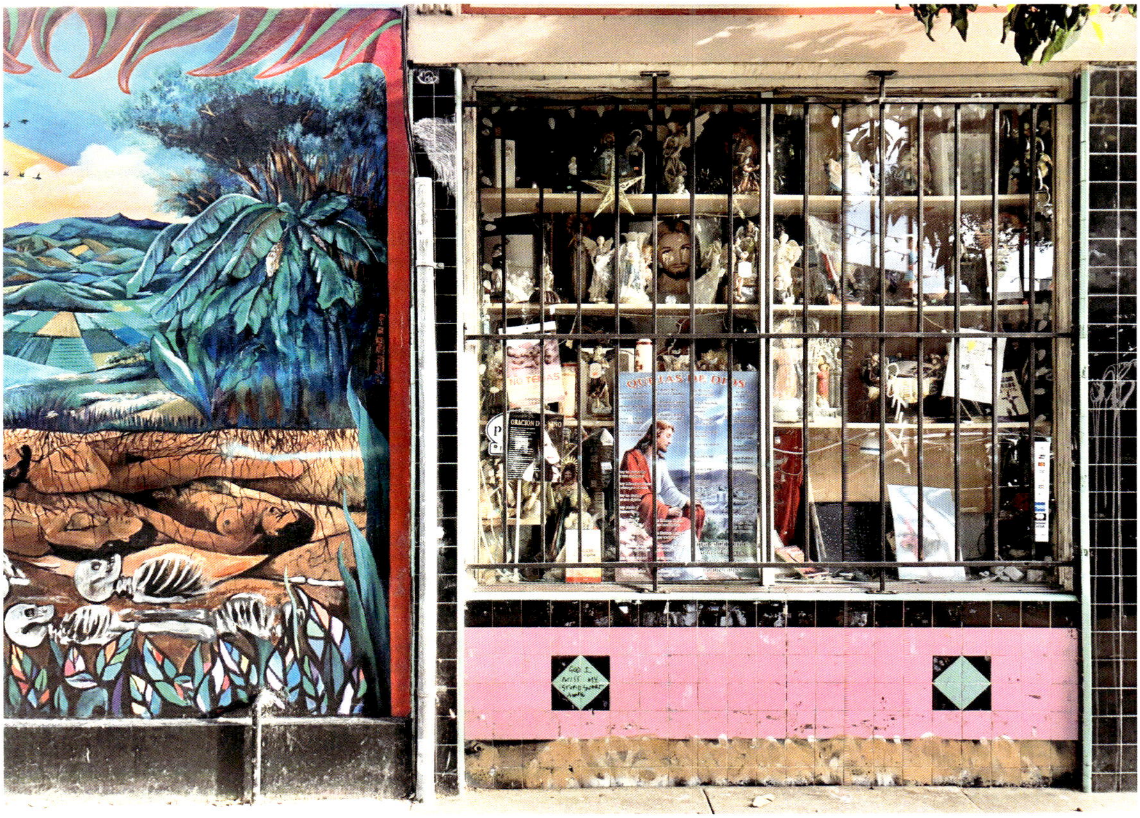

Sunday, May 31

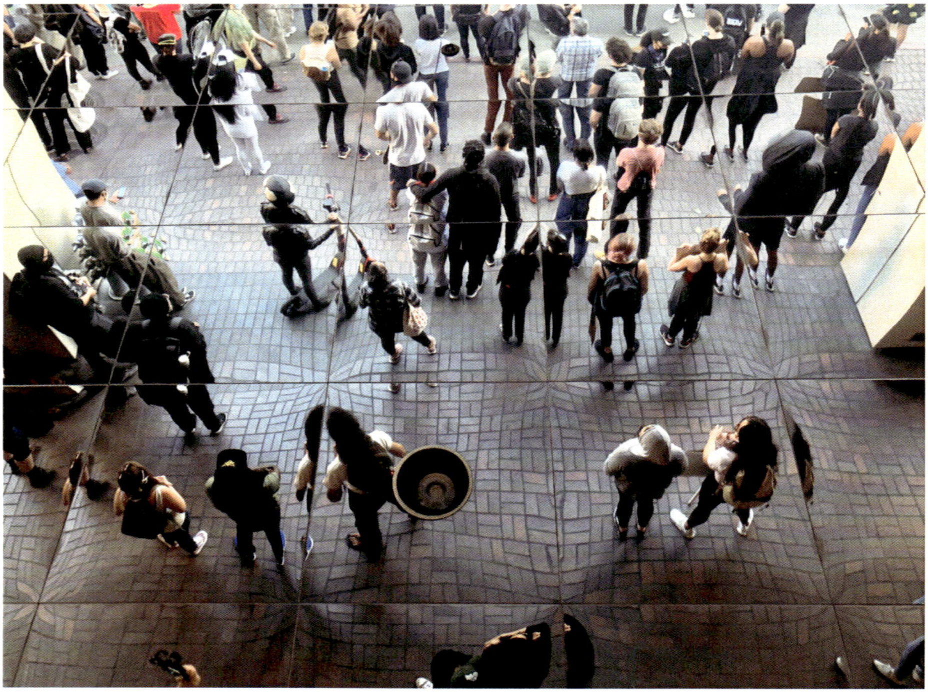

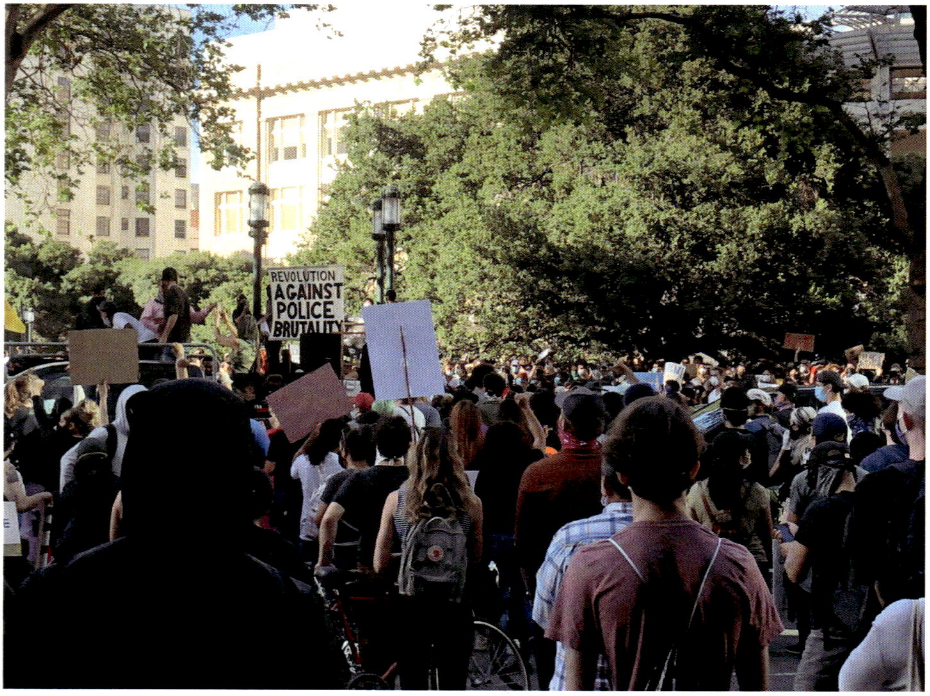
REVOLUTION
AGAINST
POLICE
BRUTALITY

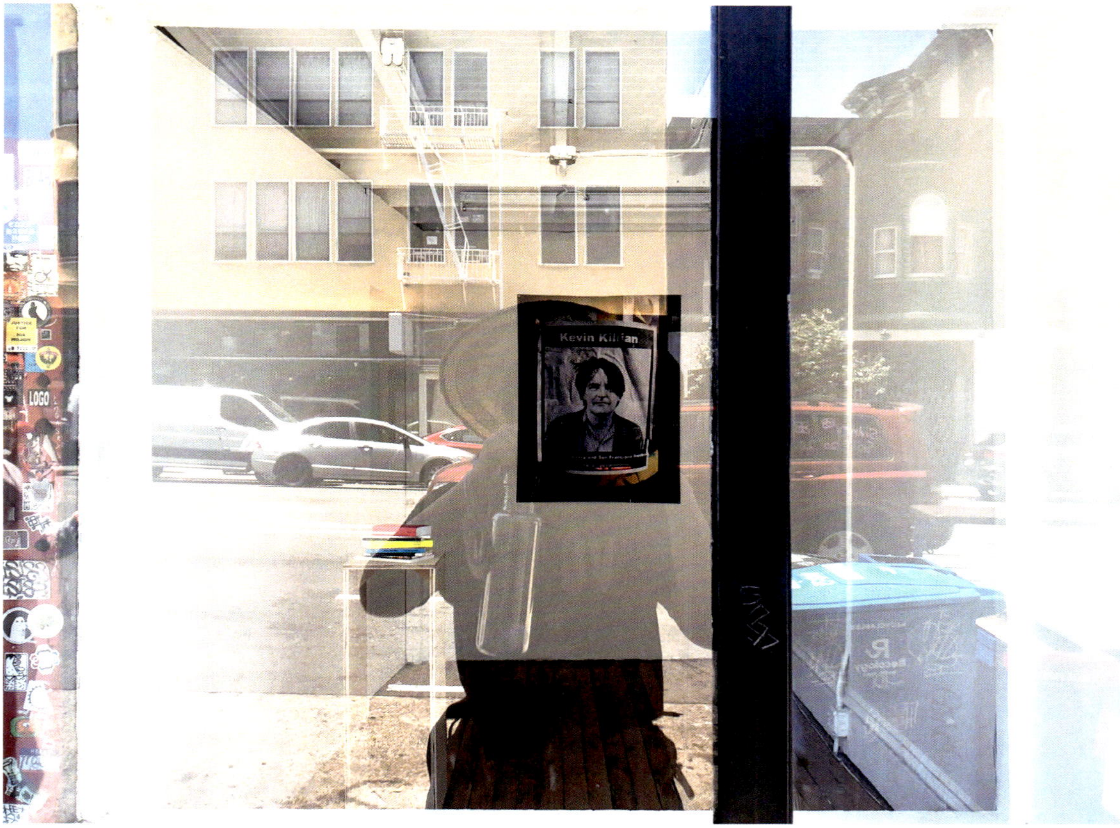

Monday, June 1

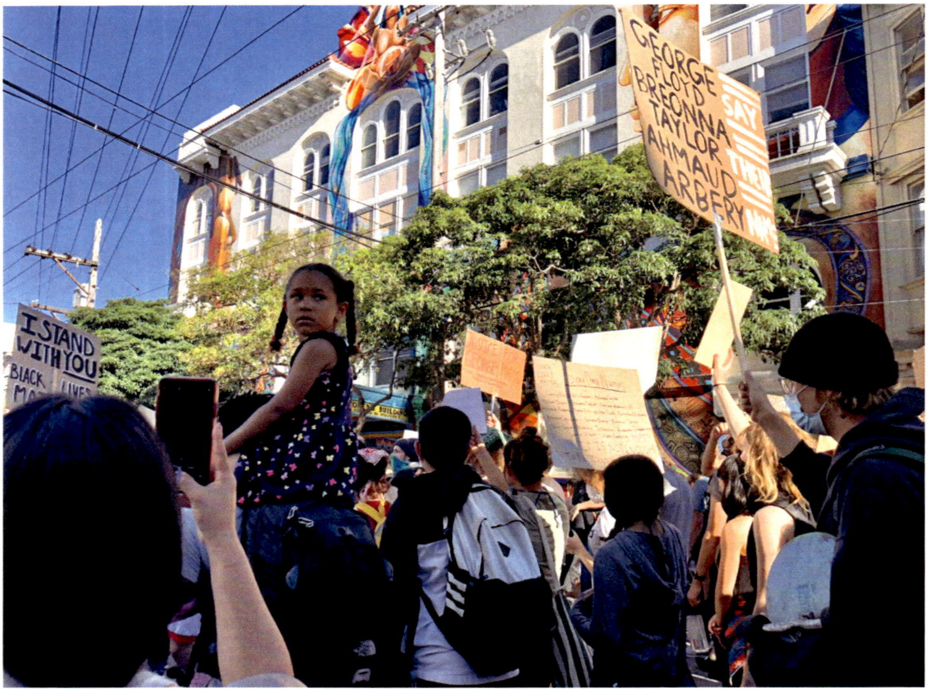
GEORGE FLOYD
BREONNA TAYLOR
AHMAUD ARBERY
I STAND WITH YOU

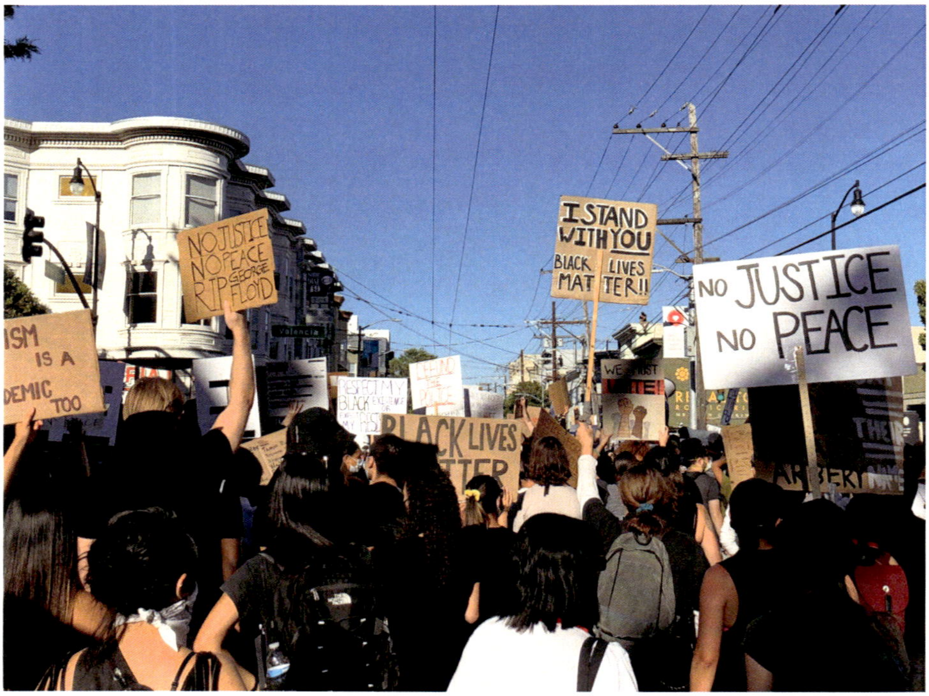
NO JUSTICE NO PEACE RIP GEORGE FLOYD
I STAND WITH YOU
BLACK LIVES MATTER!!
NO JUSTICE NO PEACE
BLACK LIVES

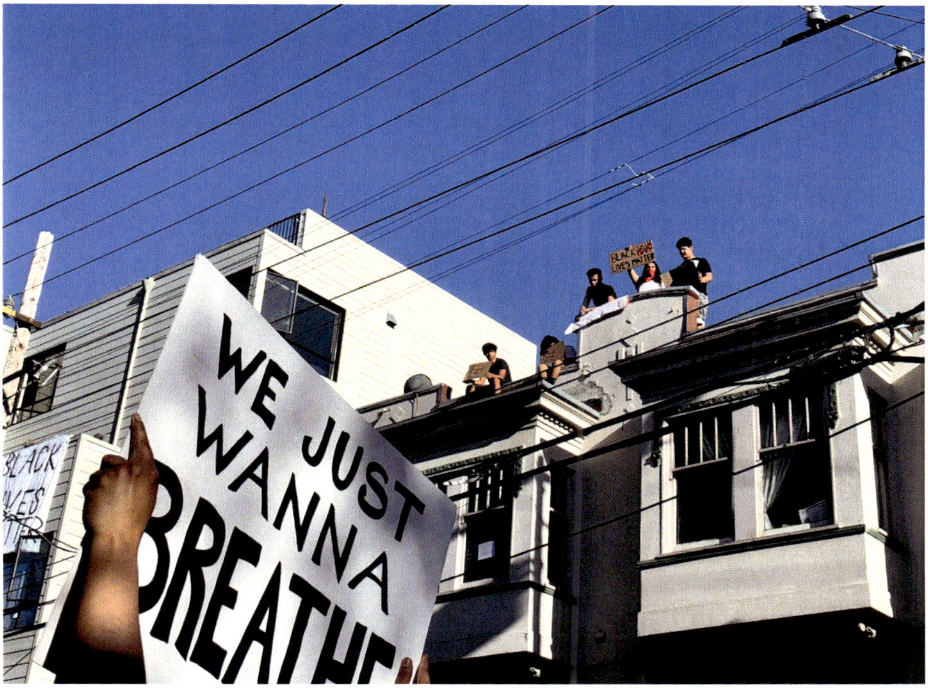

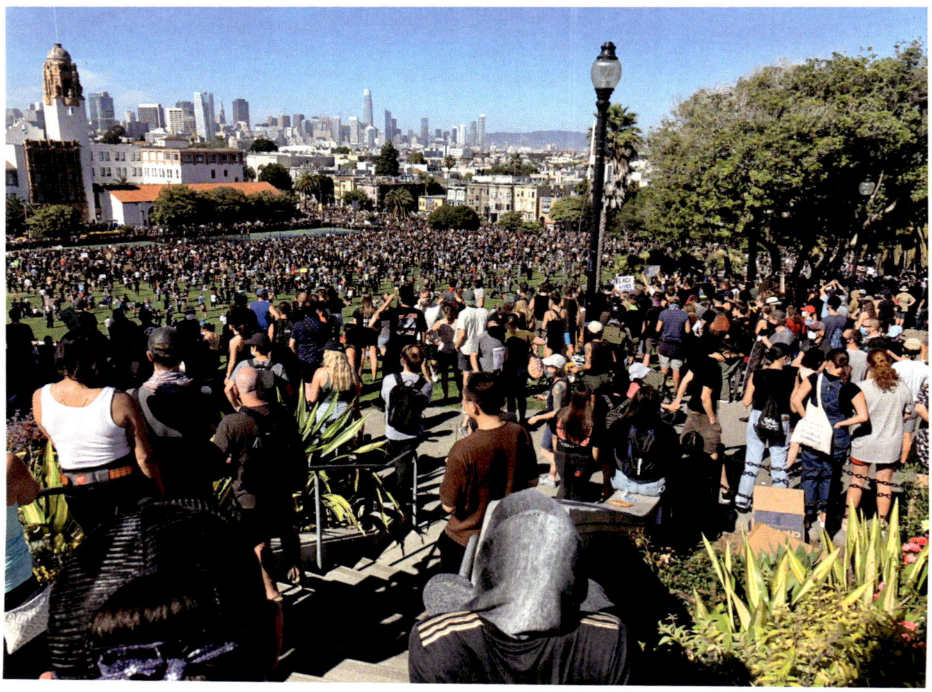

Wednesday, June 3

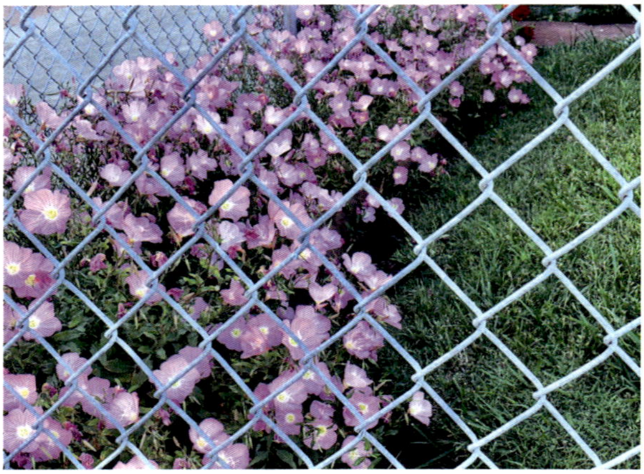

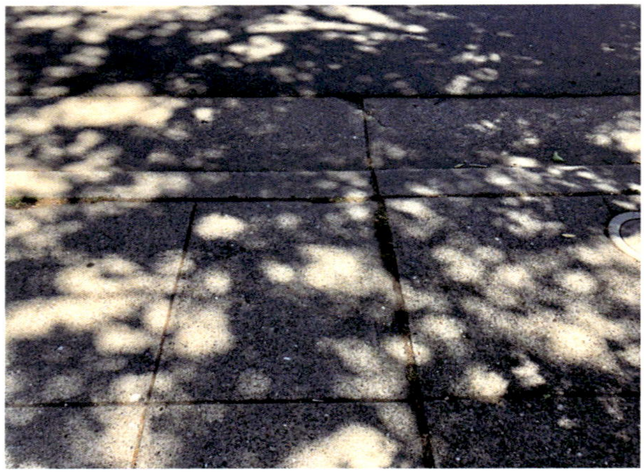

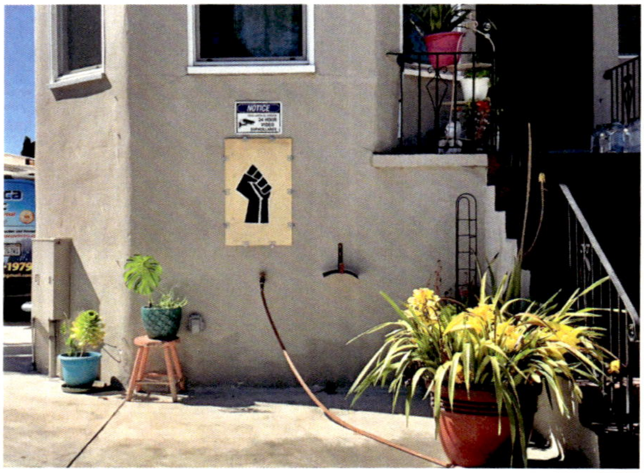

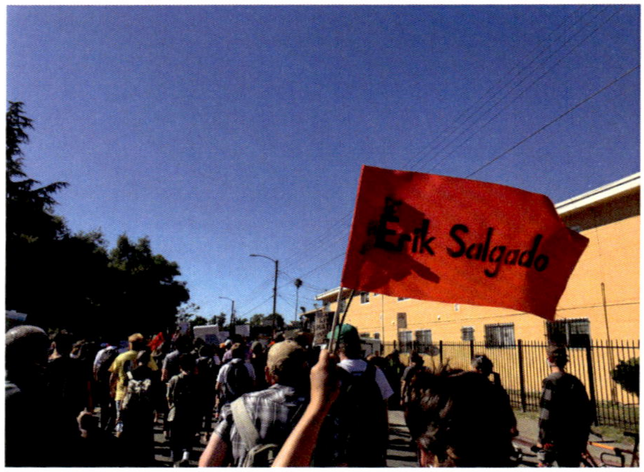
Erik Salgado

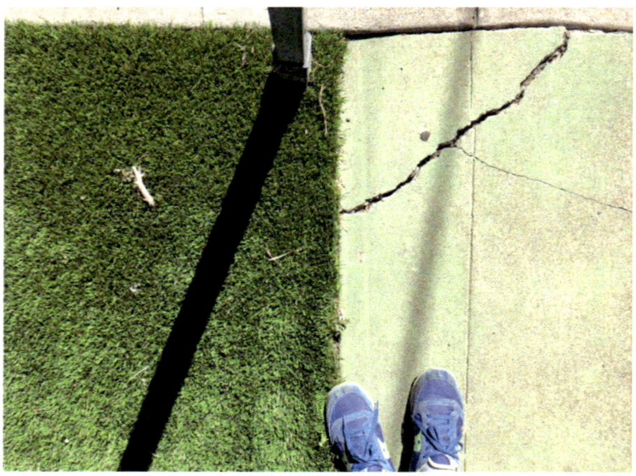

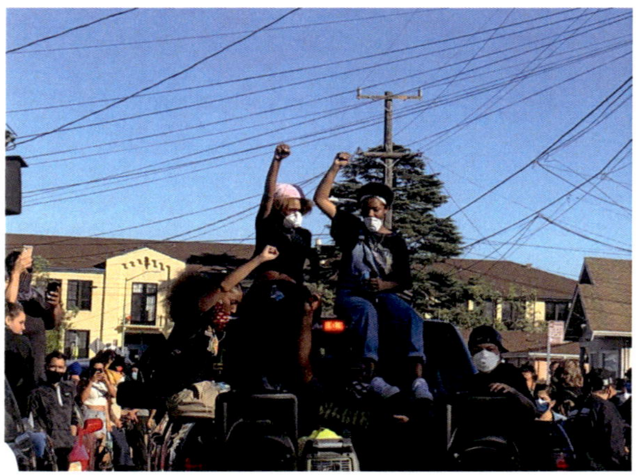

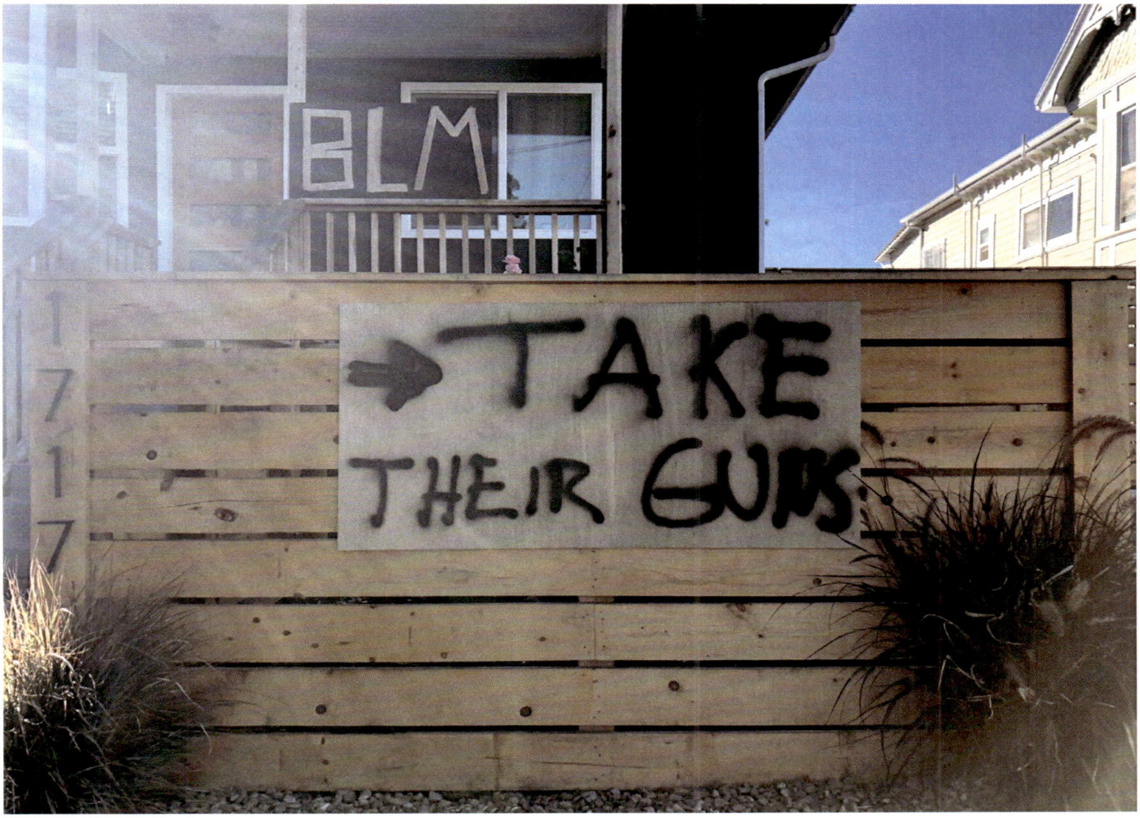

Monday, June 8

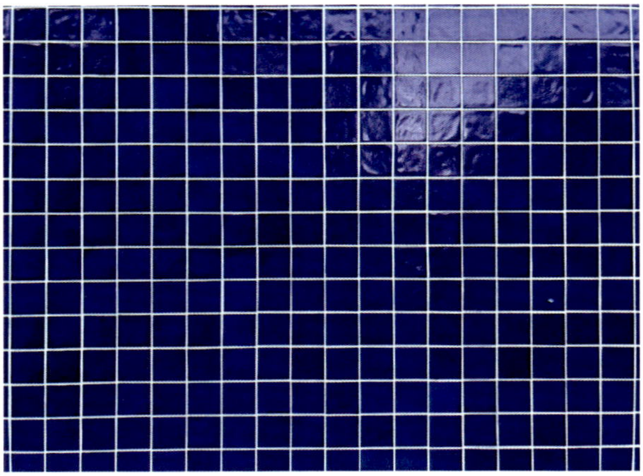

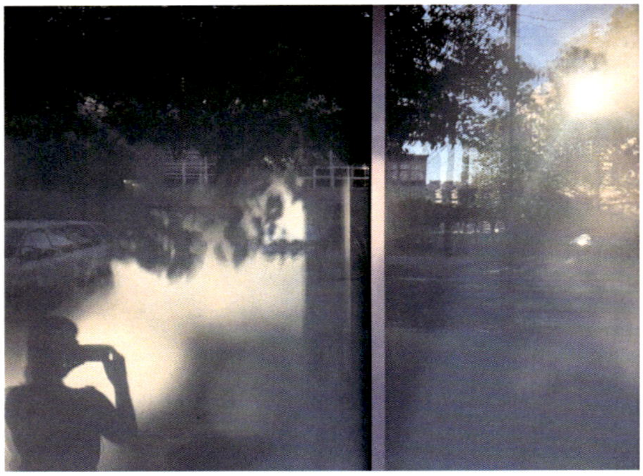

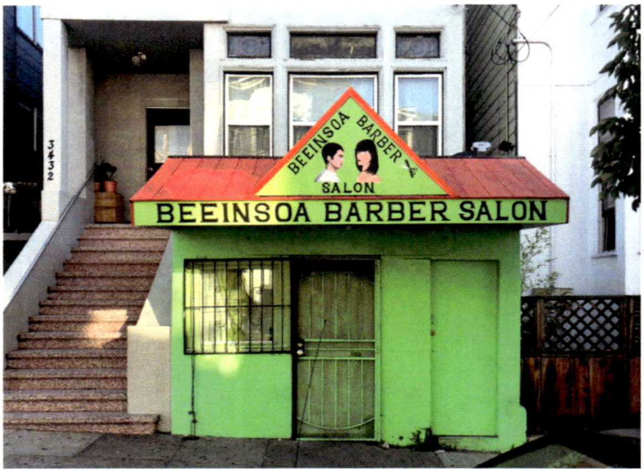
BEEINSOA BARBER
SALON
BEEINSOA BARBER SALON
3432

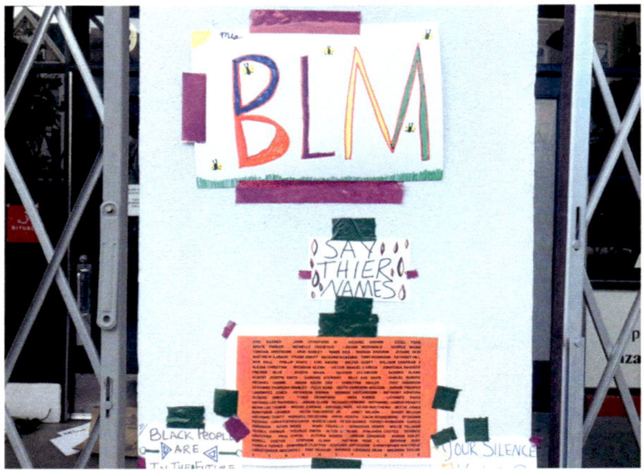
BLM
SAY THIER NAMES
BLACK PEOPLE ARE
OUR SILENCE

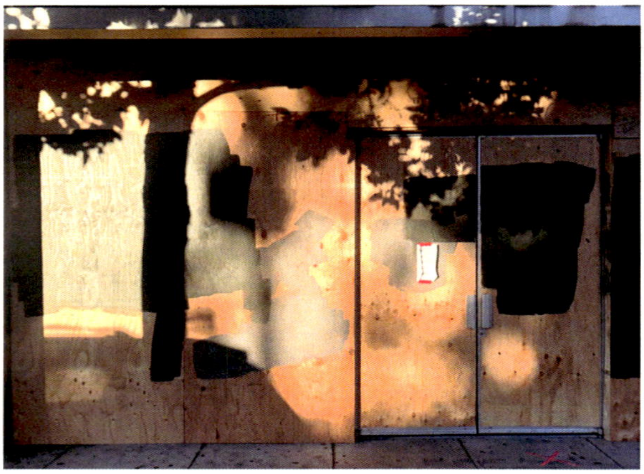

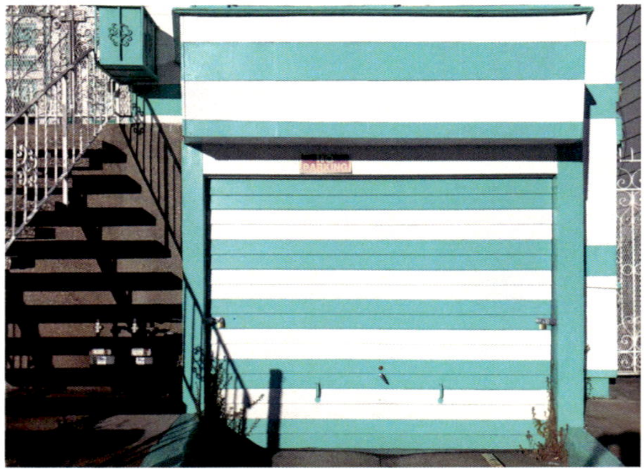

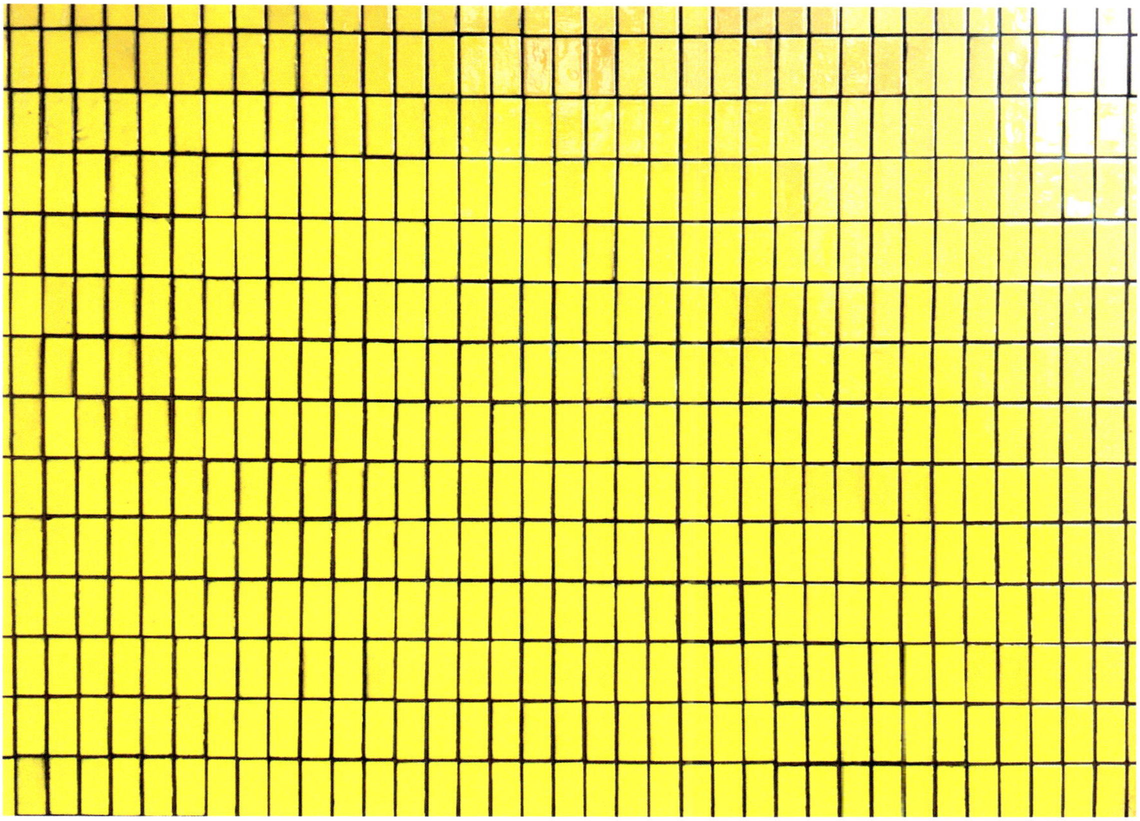

Tuesday, June 9

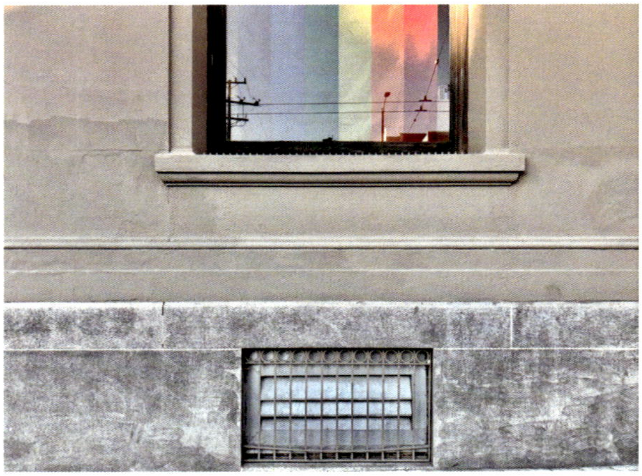

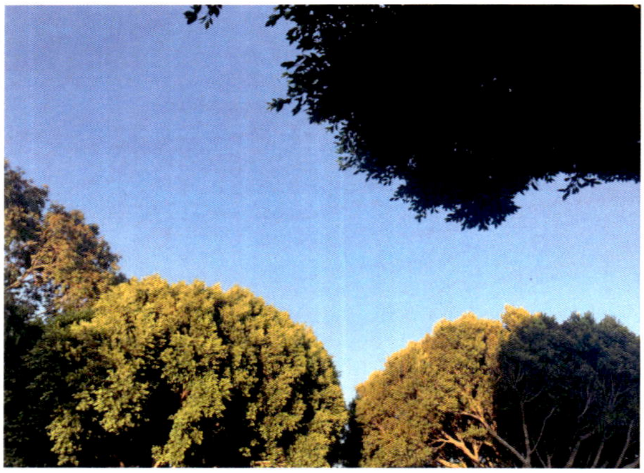

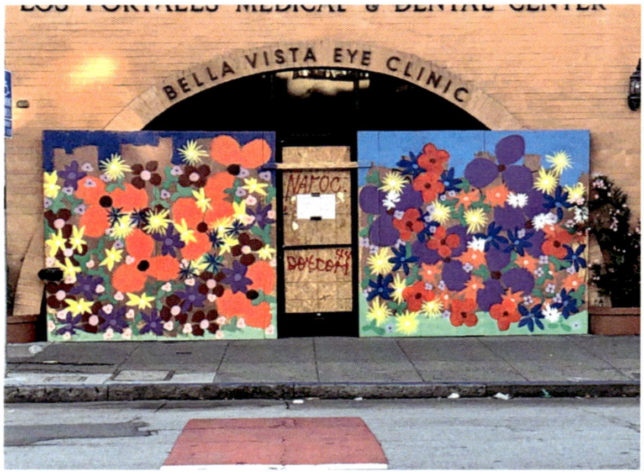
BELLA VISTA EYE CLINIC

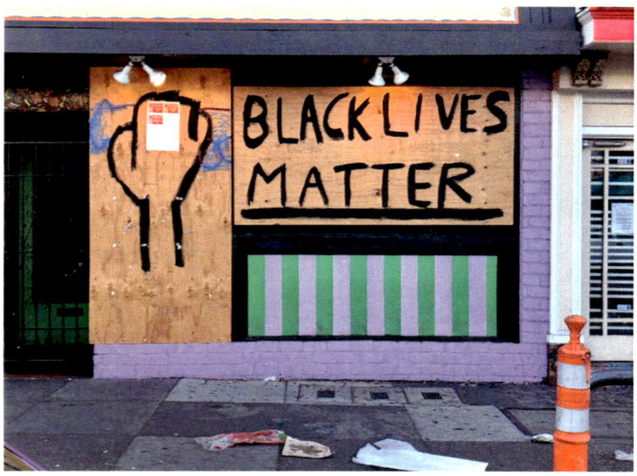
BLACK LIVES
MATTER

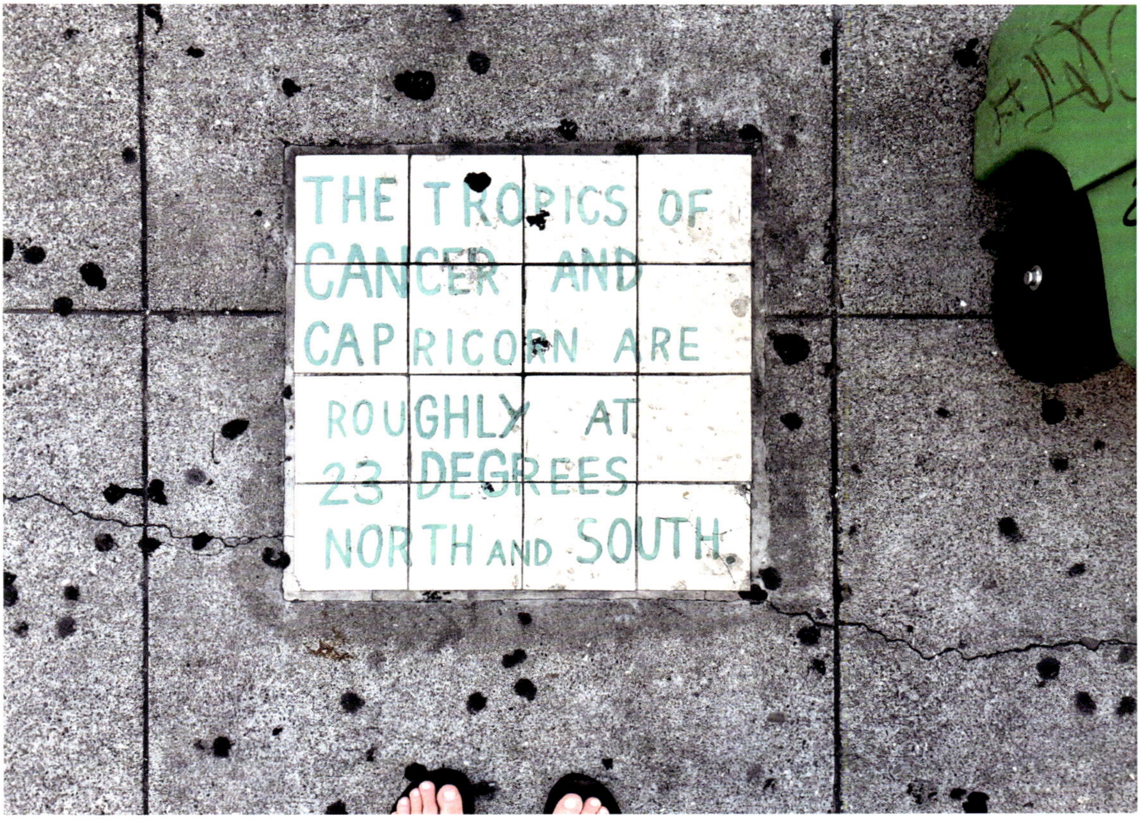

Wednesday, June 17

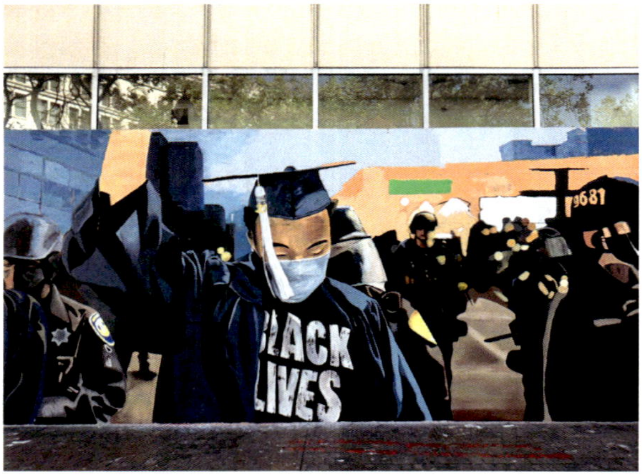
LACK
LIVES

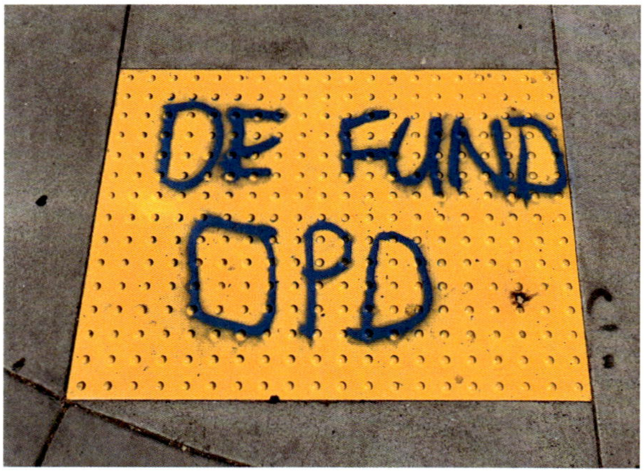
DE FUND
OPD

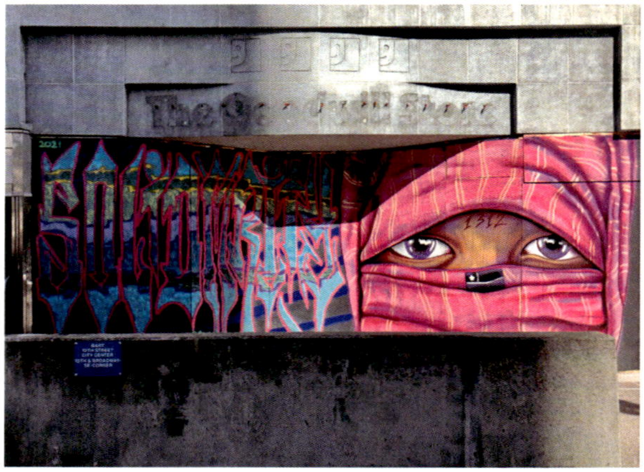

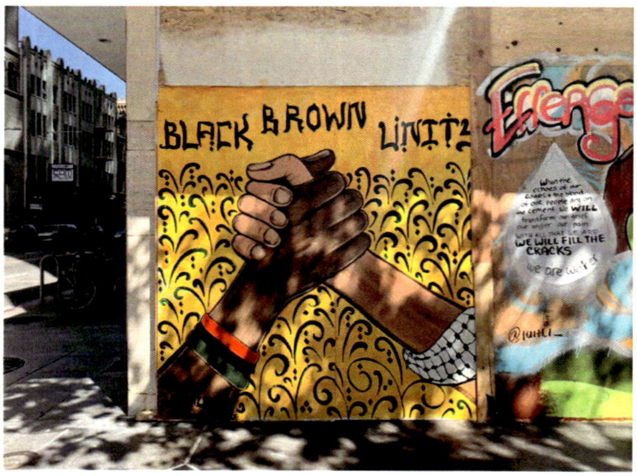
BLACK BROWN UNITE
WE WILL FILL THE CRACKS

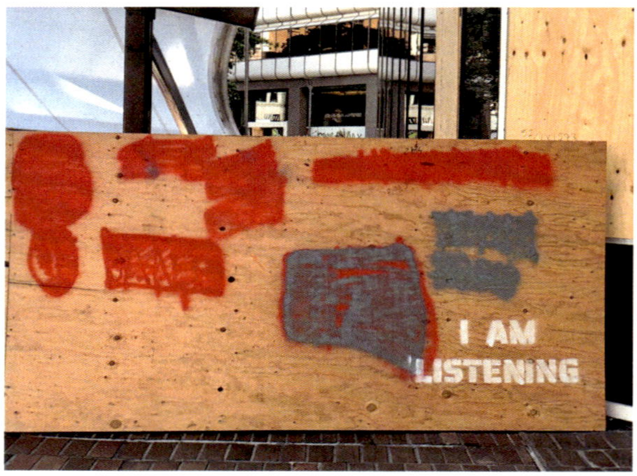
I AM
LISTENING

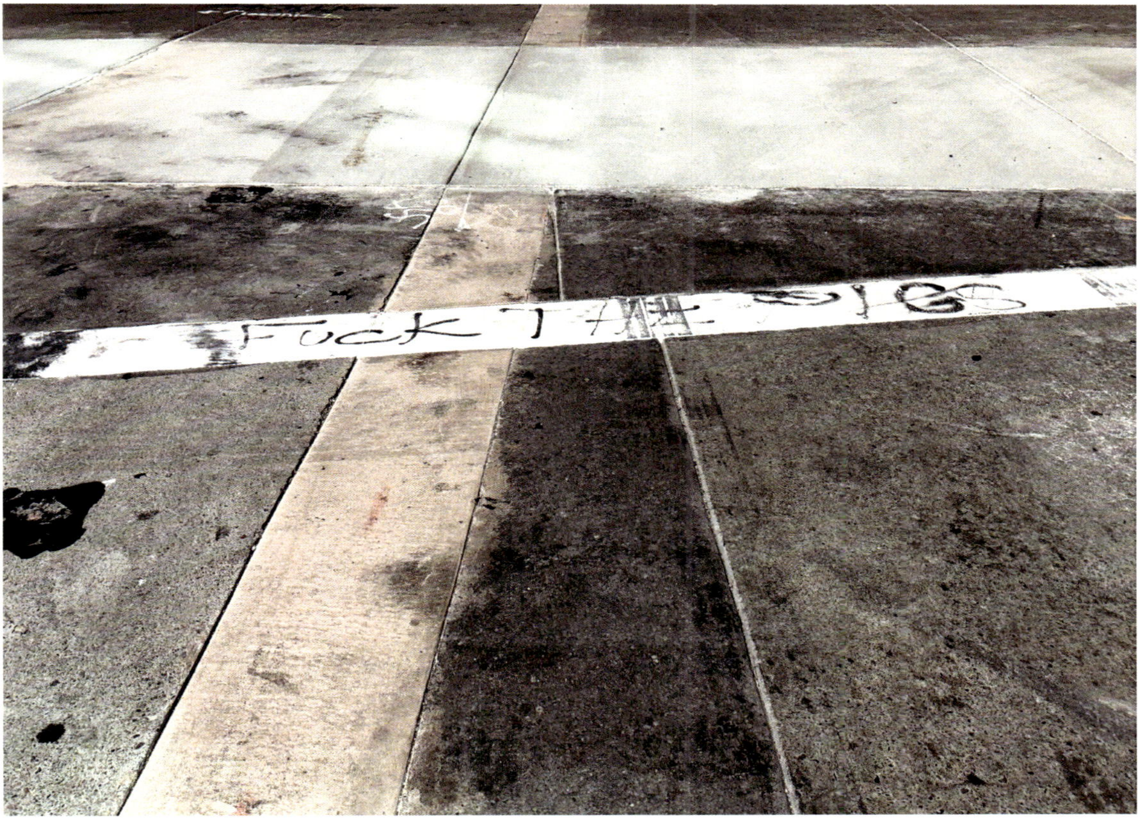

Friday, June 19

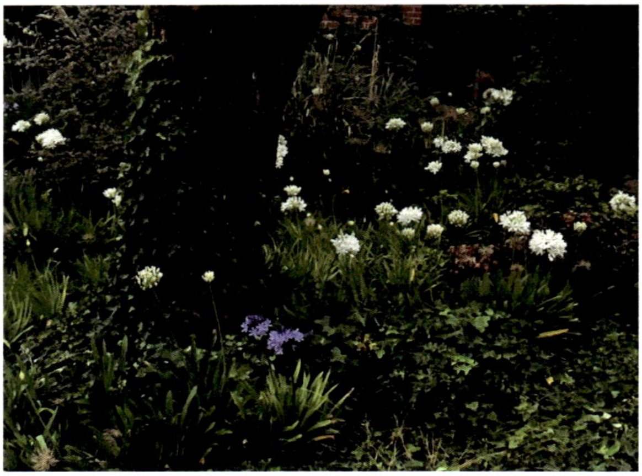
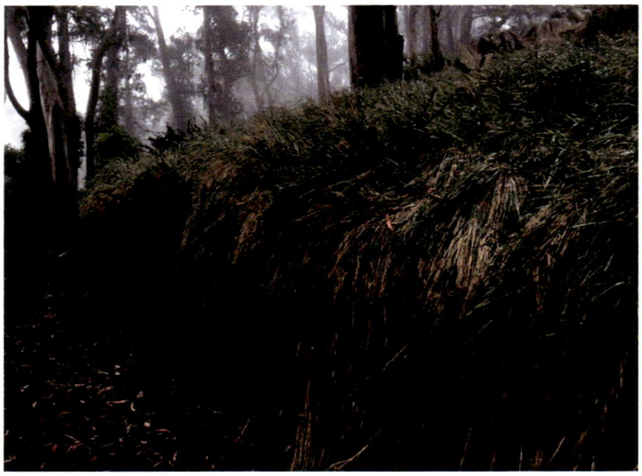
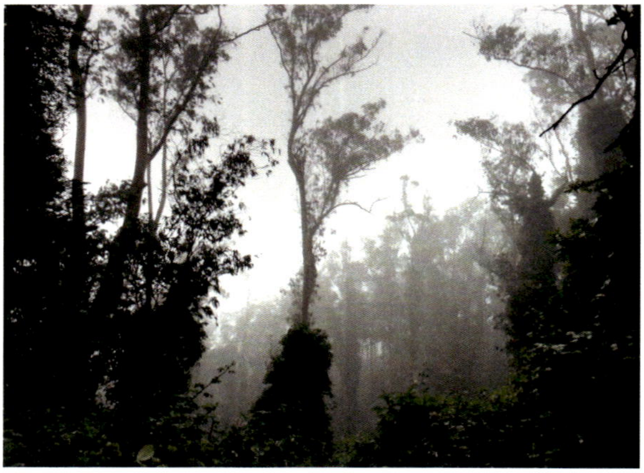
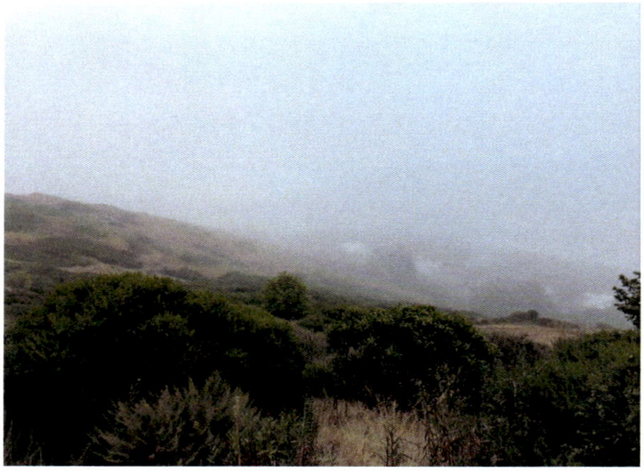
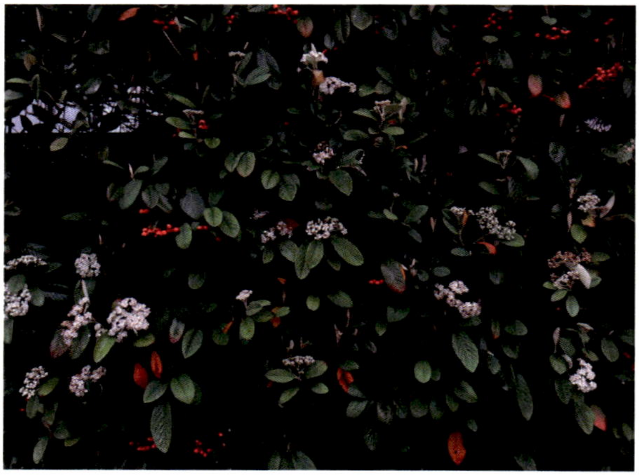
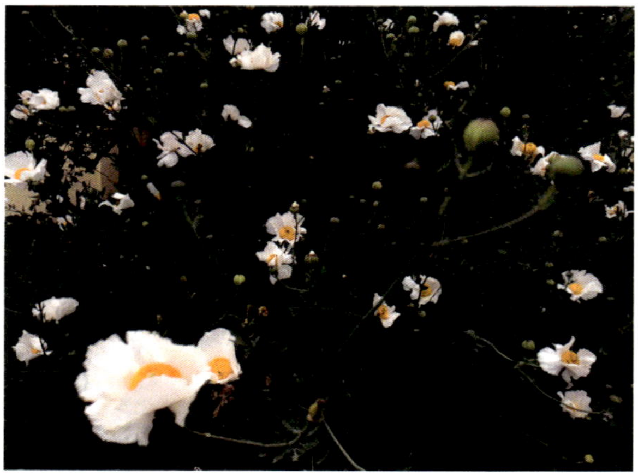

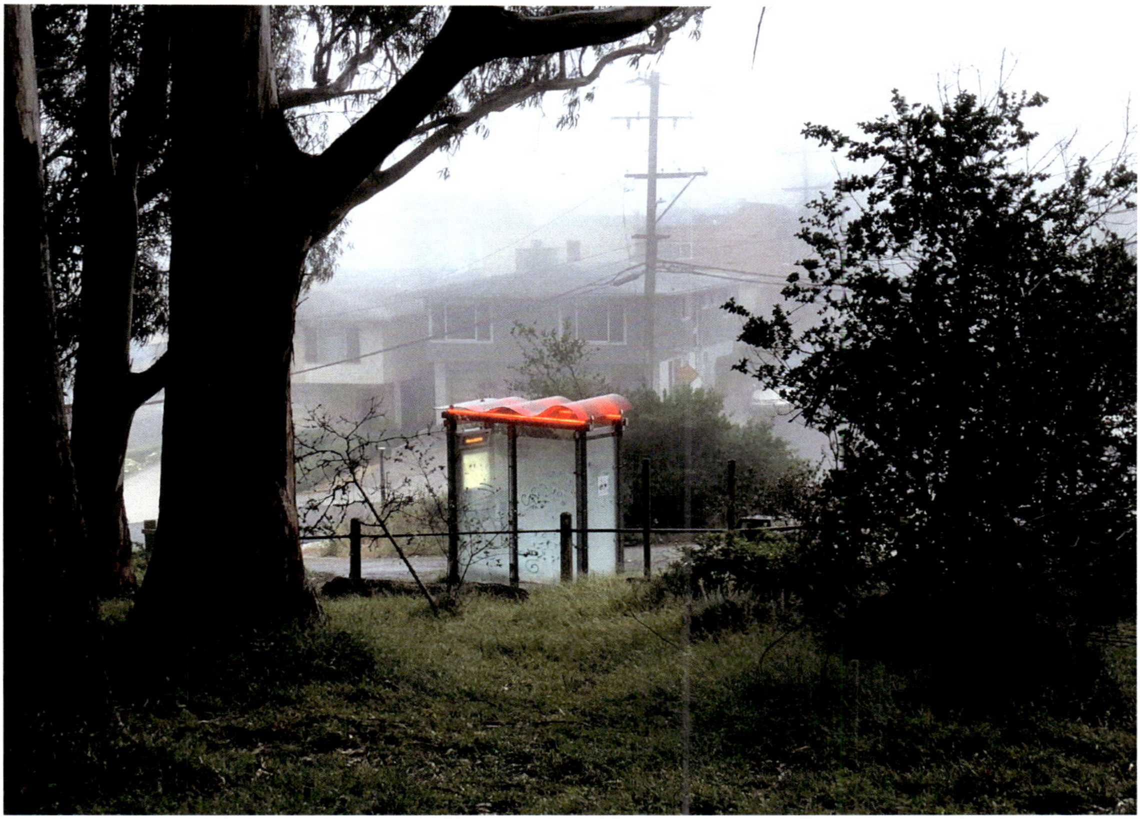

Saturday, June 20

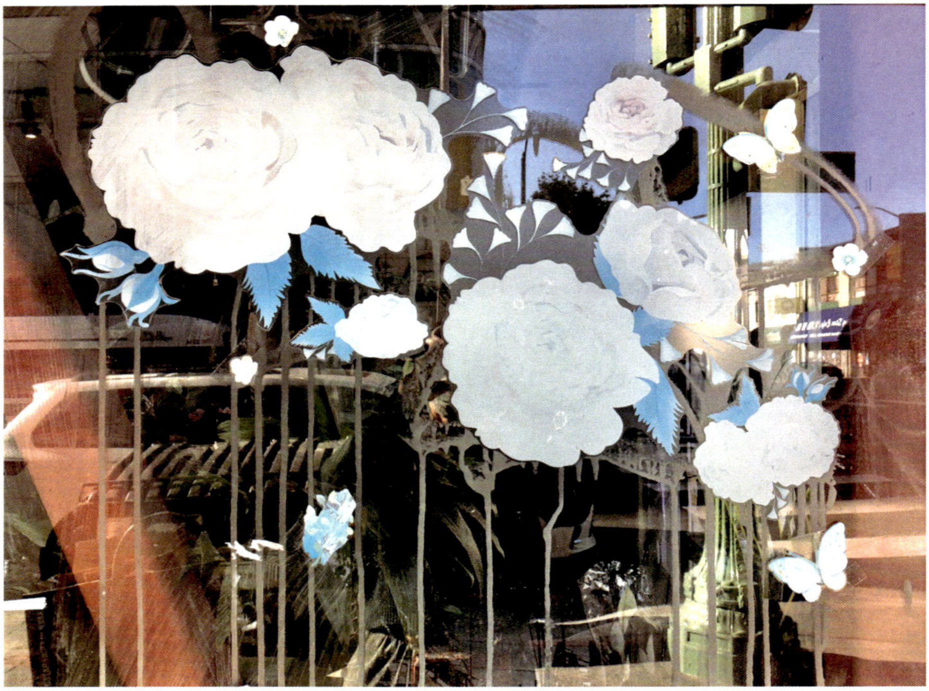

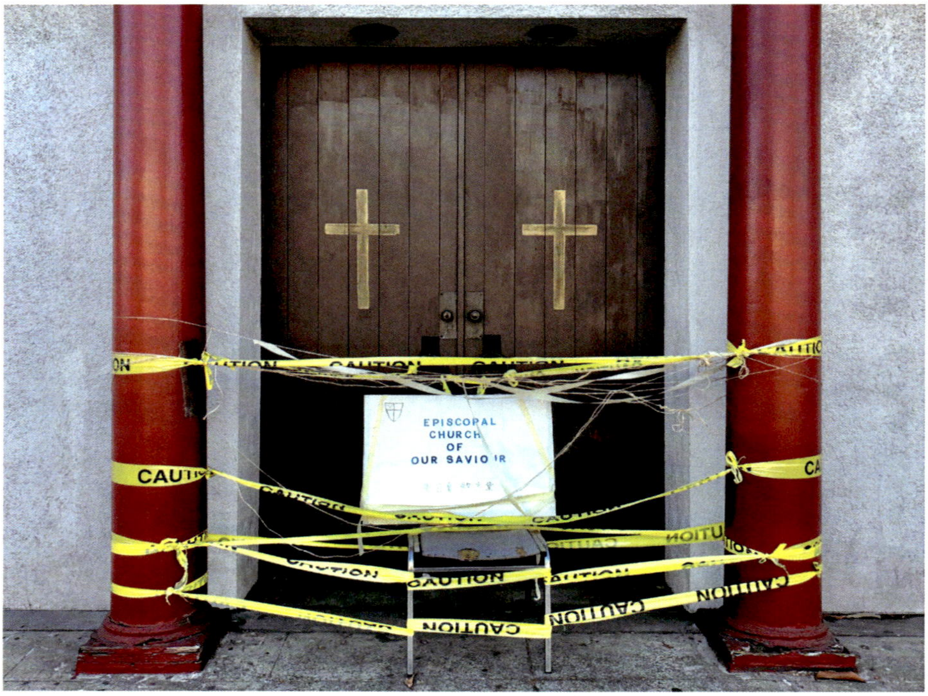
EPISCOPAL
CHURCH
OF
OUR SAVIO IR
CAUTION

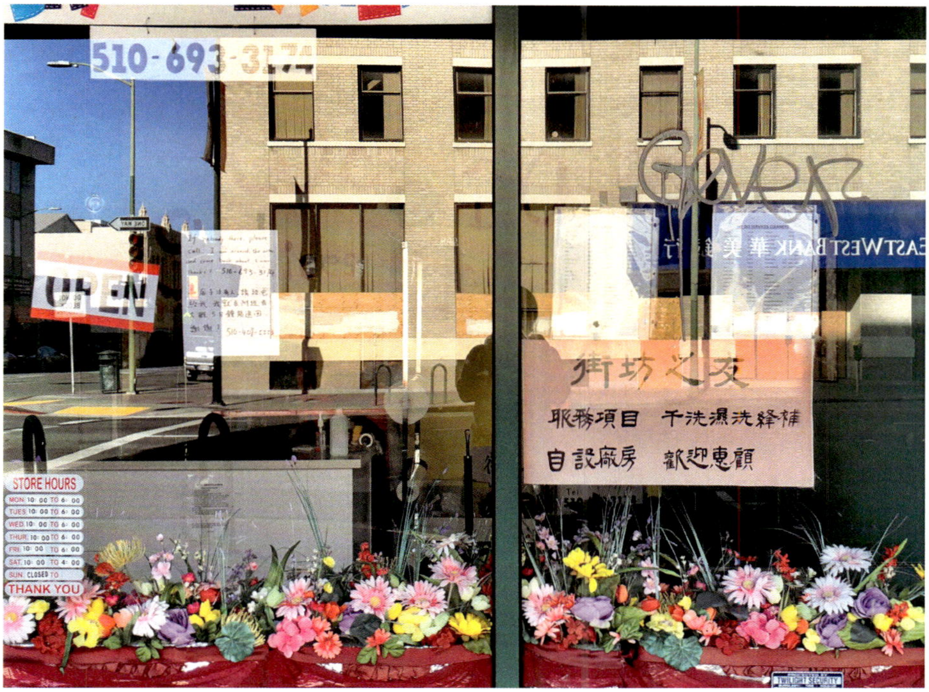

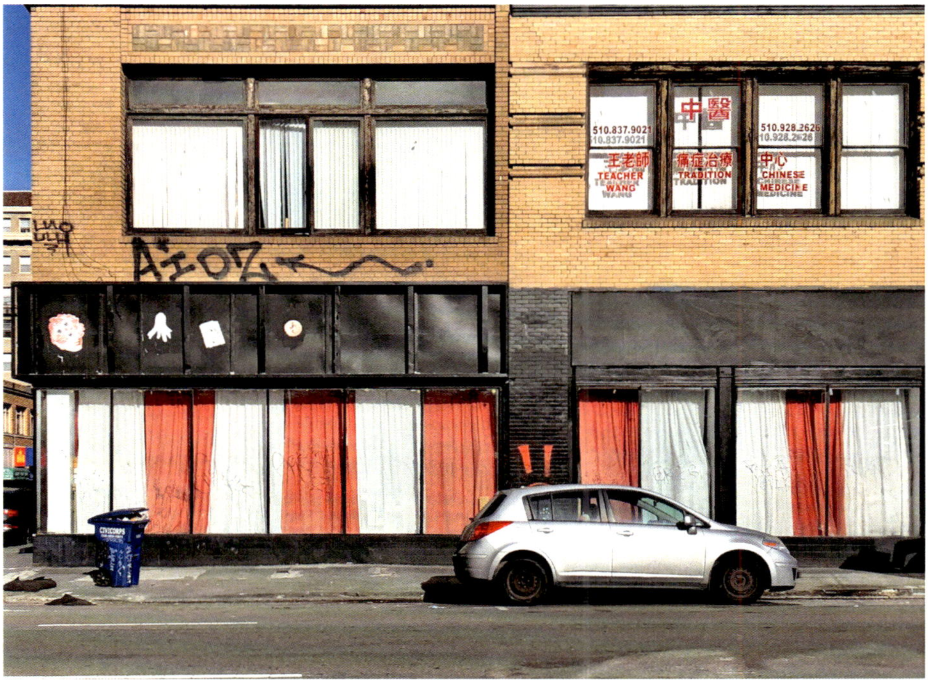

Monday, June 22

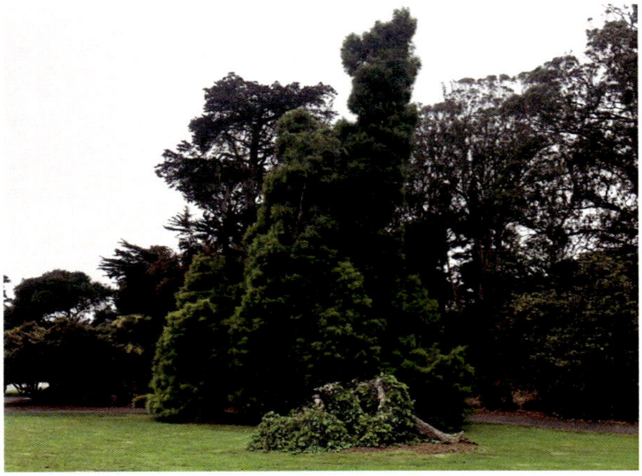

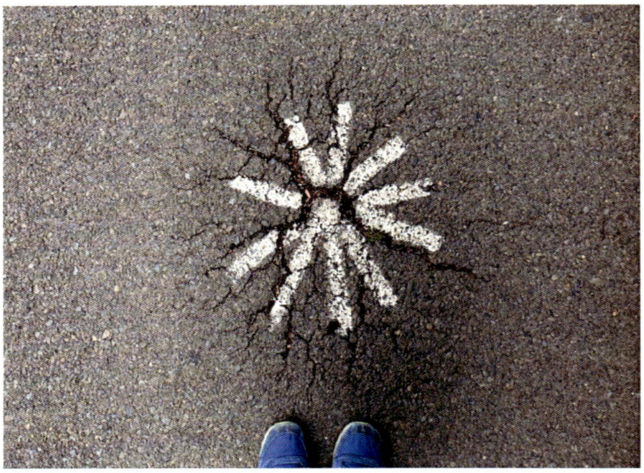

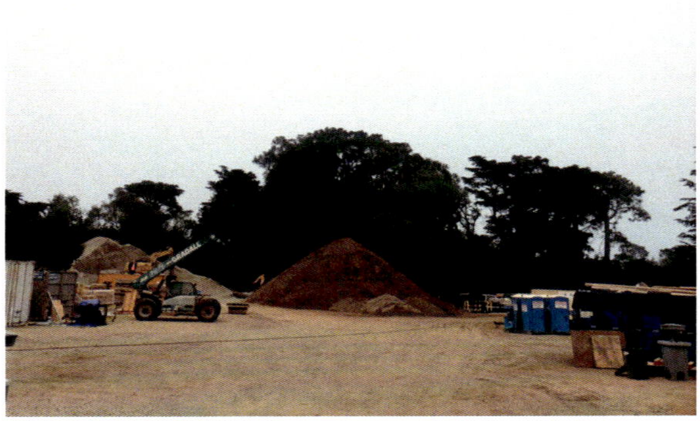

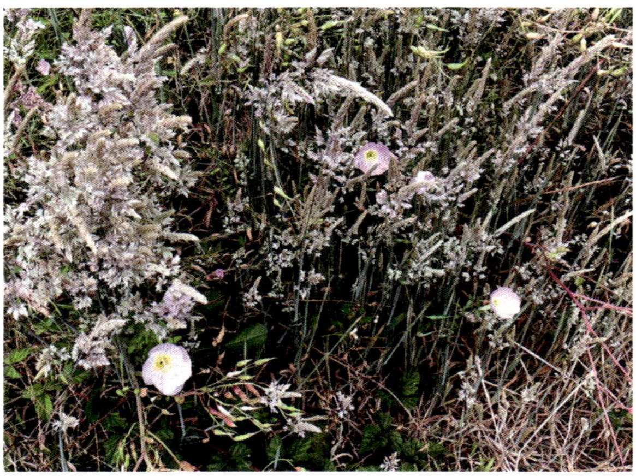

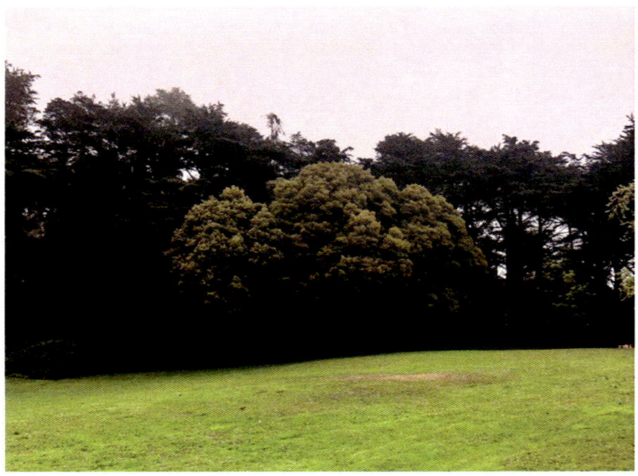

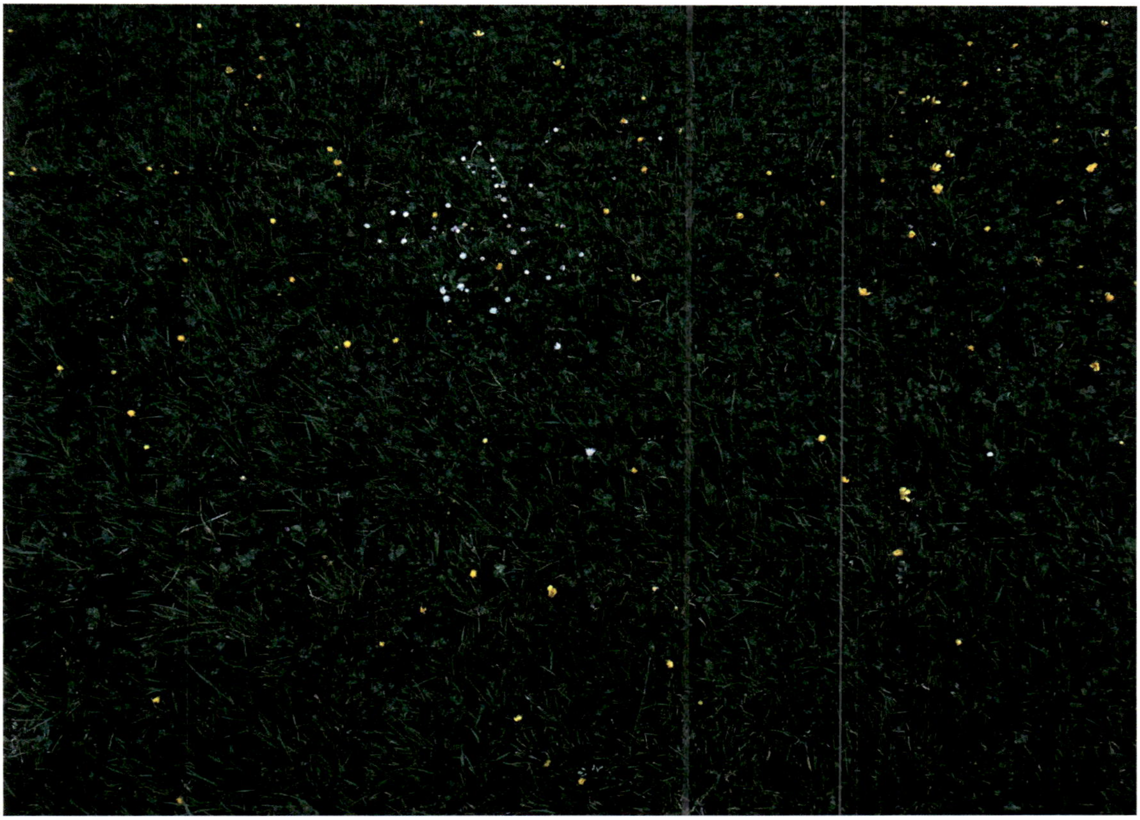

Tuesday, June 23

March 15

high up on a hill
another hill

March 20

lay a wreath
any place

there's much
to mourn

March 23

only light gets in is what

survives in rock

March 28

at the base of every palm
a crumpled colonizer

everyone and their dog
stops here to pee

the trees are stronger
the trees will win

April 4

the crack of dawn
open just a crack

and if the breeze carries me away
along with the air I'll be happy there

April 13

people don’t give weeds enough credit
being explosive and all

no truck
with enclosure

knowing what we need
before we need it

April 16

I stay signed up
for that blue

to mark a spot
to come back to

where an open
window was

April 18

the horizon is
half full

April 19

dusk throws pastels
above and beyond

whatever I think I know
in my shadow

what I like is the smudge
where my face was

light knows nothing
about “the economy”

April 20

in the dream I asked you
to open the gate

in the dream
there was no rent

April 23

what we did to the birds
and their baths was bad

a curtain on which the sun
makes love is good

it can be conceived
but not described

the longer I look at it
the longer I look at it

April 26

Anselm says
de Kooning walked

staring at the sidewalk
seeing compositions there

I try to lift my head
to develop wild theory

I abscond
in all the air among us

and something will be flying
across the sky just then

April 28

in this basket I wed
wild fennel

oxalis, datura,
California light

sycamore, sage
and umber lichen

the center of the flower
is not empty

tadpole in the gutter
tadpole in the creek

May 2

you can hear the vines
if you listen

chanting whose streets
our streets

abundant as mint
tireless as ivy

while we fuck around
going extinct

quit speaking English
to the plants

May 3

the only place for gold
is piled in the street

that's why the kids
paint rainbows there

May 7

banging my face
into the witness box

going where the rubbish
suits my shoes

May 14

the land belongs to the dead
the living and the unborn

the land does not
belong to anyone

May 18

I’ve seen a strange mass
at the end of the heart

where they keep fetishes
locked behind glass

some shatter
in seasonal rituals

a small jubilee
of proletarian shopping

it is a bit like our own custom
of splitting wishbone

May 21

I bring a dozen eggs
to my friends bereft of eggs

I place a dozen eggs on the porch
of a blue house on Essex

I move the tomato around the yard
because tomatoes don't have legs

I leave the citrus out
to dry and so too the bucket

I count myself among them
in the same sum

May 22

at night the trees
talk plotting

May 24

late in the evening
when the light was just

going away and I was done
gathering leeches for the day

May 25

a brick aloft is having
a conversation with enclosure

a burning breeze
is something to look at

the city an ember
is something to look at

May 26

by current of air
dusk turns

anything soft
thistles succumb

and lose their burl
dusk turns what

was straw to slate
never tire of this view

May 27

they broker the air
and trim into limb

they reek the water
and reek the sea

and I can’t say
I’ve ever seen a sea

but I can smell it
and you can too

it’s what death would smell like
if it had never lived

May 28

spring and them
swells what

I thought possible
there is a hole

in the air
don’t stare

May 29

a seagull
is not a symbol

there is no such thing
as private property

May 31

"the wealth of the wealthy
springs from the poverty of the poor"

the song it goes
cops and klan go hand in hand

June 1

the gravity of all these suns
and how suffused we all are

to almost appear sheer or disappear
the dead walk the street

that's my kinda mob
that's the mob I wanna be

June 3

for every pig
a pair of wings

June 8

maybe there's some
question of the number

of petals
or the placement

or definition
of the eye

but I say and sing
that pansy

down with hedges
up with pansies

of all stripes
pansies unite

June 9

panaderia over Panera

El Tonayense over Tacolicious

June 17

the calories required
to produce the fortitude

to get to *no place*
are more than the present

conditions can offer
this south facing window?

twenty two hundred
dollars a month

June 19

the town throws
light and noise

at the slats
they call windows

at the sickness
they call jail

the town throws
a fireworks show

for the people
against the police

until every last
chicken roosts

June 20

the air is dewy
where the big bloom

spreads its spokes
like a hand against the wall

the dewy hand
of a person

getting fucked or fucking
for there is no difference

the currents are circular
the air abides

I didn’t see it until
I couldn’t see any longer

June 22

fake flowers
last forever

June 23

our eyes are taken
out of the earth

see that swath?
may the scrub be unbroken

may that bed of bulbs
burst gold

Rumi Koshino is an interdisciplinary artist and educator based in San Francisco. Her intuitive process of making art is informed by everyday experiences as well as social, emotional, and political climates that surround it. She has exhibited her work in the cities along the West Coast and Japan; including the Catherine Person Gallery and Vignettes in Seattle; Right Window in San Francisco; and Sweeney Kaye Gallery and The Chetwood in Oakland. Rumi's collaborations include The Wing Luke Museum of the Asian Pacific American Experience and Prairie Underground Clothiers in Seattle. She will be a resident artist at AGA Lab in Amsterdam in 2021. She holds a BFA and an MFA from the University of Washington. She was born in Japan. (rumikoshino.com)

Alli Warren is the author of the poetry books *Little Hill* (City Lights, 2020). *I Love It Though* (Nightboat Books, 2017), and Poetry Center Book Award winner, *Here Come the Warm Jets* (City Lights, 2013). She is also the author of numerous chapbooks, including *Moveable C* (Push Press), *Don't Go Home With Your Heart On* (Faux Press), and *Grindin* (Lew Gallery). Alli edited the literary magazine *Dreamboat*, co-curated the (New) Reading Series at 21 Grand, contributed to SFMOMA's *Open Space*, and co-edited the Poetic Labor Project. Her writing has appeared in many publications, including *Harpers, Poetry, The Brooklyn Rail*, and *BOMB*. She has performed her work widely, including internationally in Canada, England, Iceland, and Mexico. Alli has lived and worked in the Bay Area since 2005.

Robin Wright co-founded RITE Editions in 2007 in San Francisco with the intent of commissioning artists to make limited edition publications. Since its inception, RITE Editions has published 23 editions. Every RITE Edition is produced in close collaboration with each respective artist and writer, and is distinguished by its conceptual nature. (riteeditions.com)

Printed in the United States of America

First Edition

ISBN 978-0-9975843-3-2

Design & Typesetting: Margaret Tedesco
Printed by Edition One, Berkeley

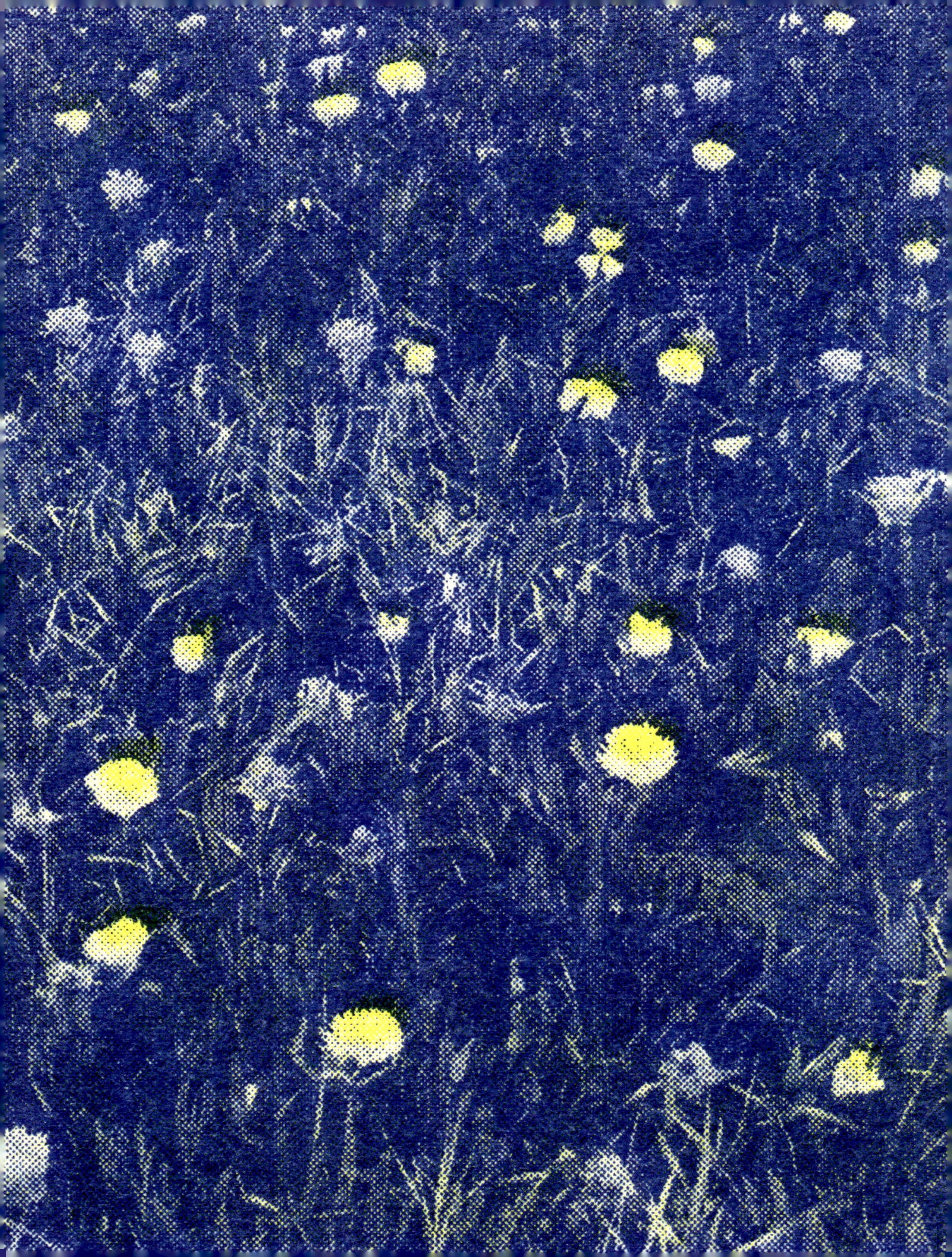